# *Bible Gems*

## *Volume I*

### By Bill Delperdange

Lighthouse Baptist Church
170 Becnel Lane
Shepherdsville, KY, USA 40165

Preserving Our Baptist History

Preserving Our Baptist History Press

**Contact Info:** preserving.our.baptist.history@gmail.com

All Scripture is from the King James Bible.

Preserving Our Baptist History

ISBN (Paperback): 9798306400730
ISBN (Hardcover): 9798306400808
First Edition: January 2025

# Table of Contents

# Introduction: What are Bible Gems?

*"Hello! And welcome to Bible Gems on WIOP, 95.1 fm. I'm Brother Bill from Lighthouse Baptist Church at 170 Becnel Lane in Shepherdsville."* These are the words I always use to start my short radio program, *"Bible Gems,"* on Lighthouse Christian Radio, WIOP, at 95.1 fm. In my first broadcast, I explained what Bible Gems are and how you can find some of your own! Bible Gems are just special truths that God reveals to us. He makes them stand out as we do our personal study of Scripture. It is a truth or an idea that speaks to us in a special way. We ordinarily do not find these through casually reading the Scriptures but rather through careful study. 2 Timothy 2:15 admonishes us to *"Study to show thyself approved unto God, a workman that needeth not to be ashamed, rightly dividing the word of truth."* This type of study takes effort and digs more deeply into the Scripture than just reading does. It allows us to understand more fully what God is telling us. It is only then that we can expect the Lord to give us these gems buried deep within its pages. In this book I will share with you some of the gems that God has given me. In so doing, I hope to encourage you to dig into the Bible to find the gems that God has hidden there for you! Here are the manuscripts of the original 52 Bible Gems that I recorded for the radio station. I have put them in a form that could be used as a devotional book if you choose. I have also added some pictures from my travels around the world. I hope you enjoy them! Happy digging!

# 1 – My Redeemer Liveth

Some people believe that salvation in the Old Testament was obtained in a different way than in the New Testament. This view, however, does not agree with Scripture. Scholars tell us that the book of Job is the oldest book in the Bible. The book of Genesis records earlier events and may be based on older documents, but was put in its present form by Moses at a time that was likely later than Job. We find today's Bible Gem in Job 19:25-27 where Job says, "*25For I know that my redeemer liveth, and that he shall stand at the latter day upon the earth: 26And though after my skin worms destroy this body, yet in my flesh shall I see God: 27Whom I shall see for myself, and mine eyes shall behold, and not another; though my reins be consumed within me.*" Job lived about the same time as the patriarch, Abraham, and yet he understood that he needed a Redeemer to save him. He believed that this Redeemer would come to Earth at a later time in history. He believed that though one day he (Job) would die, that he would then be physically resurrected to stand before God. The Redeemer that Job was looking to is revealed to us in the New Testament as the Lord Jesus Christ. Job was looking forward to His coming to redeem fallen man, whereas we look back to when the Lord actually did come to Earth to die for our sins. Salvation has always been by the grace of God through faith in the shed blood of Jesus Christ on Calvary. Some of the Old Testament saints had clearer understandings of this than others, but whether in clear knowledge or acceptance of Him through the pictures given them in the many sacrifices of Israel, they were all saved through faith. *"Neither is there salvation in any other: for there is none other name under heaven given among men, whereby we must be saved."* Acts 4:12.

The Garden Tomb, Jerusalem, Israel, June 2007

# 2 – Pool of Bethesda

I was studying through the book of John and wanted to gain a better understanding of the Lord's healing of the blind man at the pool of Bethesda. As I read through John chapter 5, I read quickly through the first two verses in order to get to the details of the actual miracle. I immediately realized that I had basically skipped over two verses of Scripture as *"unimportant"* and went back and reread them. What I found there is one of my favorite Bible Gems. Verse 2 says, *"Now there is at Jerusalem by the sheep market a pool, which is called in the Hebrew tongue Bethesda, having five porches."* From previous studies, I knew that the pool's name, Bethesda, means *"House of Grace"* in Hebrew. What I noticed this time was that this pool was situated near the *"sheep market!"* I thought to myself, why would the Lord mention a detail like that? Then I considered the purpose of the sheep market in Jerusalem…to provide the lambs to be sacrificed in the Temple! The sheep market was the *"place of the sacrifice."* In John 1:29, John says of the Lord Jesus, *"…Behold the Lamb of God, which taketh away the sin of the world!"* The Lord Jesus is the Lamb that was slain on the cross for our sins that we might have the grace and forgiveness of God. The *"House of Grace"* is beside the *"place of the sacrifice"* because there is no grace of God without the sacrifice of the Lord Jesus! If you have not yet trusted in Christ and received God's grace, let me encourage you to do so today! Romans 10:13 promises,

*"For whosoever shall call upon the name of the LORD shall be saved."* Just admit you are a guilty sinner, trust that Jesus' blood on the cross was the only thing that could and does pay for your sin, ask Christ to come into your heart and forgive you, and you can be saved today! ...Then stop by and let us know that you got saved! Keep studying the Word and before long you will be finding your own Bible Gems!

Antonia Fortress, Jerusalem, Israel, June 2007

# 3 – The Righteousness of Christ (Two Halves of Salvation)

Today's Bible Gem comes from 2 Corinthians 5:21, which says, *"For he hath made him to be sin for us, who knew no sin; that we might be made the righteousness of God in him."* The He in this verse refers to God, the Father, and the Him refers, of course, to the Lord Jesus Christ; the only One to ever live a perfect life here on Earth. The Lord Jesus is the Author and Provider of our salvation! I have often heard preaching that speaks of the truth expressed in the first part of this verse, the fact that the Lord Jesus died for our sins…as our perfect and sinless sacrifice to take away our sins! We only need to trust Him by faith to be saved. I frequently preach this myself! This is one of the most important truths for us to understand in life…but it is only half of what Christ has done for us and without both halves, the equation would be incomplete, and we would be no closer to Heaven than before we accepted Christ. If all Christ had done is take away our sins, our account would be back to zero, but He did much more than that for us. Not only was Christ our Substitute in death, but He was our Substitute in life as well. He took our place in living the perfect life that we never could! The last part of our verse today says, *"…that we might be made the righteousness of God in him."* We not only needed our sins washed away by His perfect blood and sacrifice, but we also needed His righteousness in its place to be accepted in the Father's sight. Christ took away our sins. This was the negative transaction. …But He also gave us His perfect righteousness! This is the positive transaction, so that we too can be pleasing in the sight of God! We are justified, not by our own righteousness, but by His righteousness being applied to our account!

The Torah at the Western Wall, Jerusalem, Israel, June 2007

# 4 – Daniel's Prayer of Repentance

Today's Bible Gem comes from Daniel chapter 9. This chapter is the prayer that Daniel prayed while the nation of Israel was held captive in Babylon under the reign of Darius of Persia. I call it Daniel's Prayer of Repentance. Daniel was a righteous man. That is not to say that he was perfect, because only the Lord Jesus Christ is perfect. Romans 3:23 declares, *"For all have sinned, and come short of the glory of God."* Daniel was a sinner like the rest of us, but he lived a very godly life. Daniel lived such a good life that when his enemies tried to accuse him in Daniel 6:5, they said, *"We shall not find any occasion against this Daniel, except we find it against him concerning the law of his God."* Did you catch that? The only thing they could accuse him of was that obeyed God when they made it illegal to do so. So, then this good man, Daniel, begins to pray to God for himself and his nation. In Daniel 9:3 we read, *"And I set my face unto the Lord God, to seek by prayer and supplications, with fasting, and sackcloth, and ashes."* The prayer he prays lasts from verse 4 through verse 19 of this chapter. From the very beginning of the prayer, we notice something very unusual and important. When Daniel prays, he confesses the sins of Israel as his own. He never says what they have done or what Israel has done, but rather says we or I throughout the chapter. He claims the sins of his nation as his own. He does not blame anyone else despite the fact that he had not personally committed any of the offences that he is confessing! In every single verse from verse 5 through 16, Daniel confesses, *"We have sinned"* and *"We have obeyed not"* and *"We have not hearkened."* He took full responsibility for the sins of his nation and God heard and answered that prayer! This precious gem should instruct us in how to pray for our nation! Wickedness is rampant across the land and spiritually the days are growing darker and more dangerous. If we want God to do something in our homes and in our churches and in our nation, we need to pray as Daniel did. Instead of praying about God dealing with the sins of others in our nation, we must take responsibility for them and confess these sins as if they were our own. In 2 Chronicles 7:14, God says, *"If my people, which are called by my name, shall humble themselves, and pray, and seek my face, and turn from their wicked ways; then will I hear from heaven, and will forgive their sin, and will heal their land."* If we want to see God work in our nation again, we need to be on our faces before him and confess the sins of our nation. I, for one, do not believe it is too late to see God move in our nation again! Let us be on our faces before Him every day confessing our country's sins and pleading for His intervention in these last days! Let us see God work mightily once again!

# 5 – Names in Ruth

I do not believe a person needs to know Greek or Hebrew to understand the Word of God, but sometimes a little study of specific words in those languages can add some color to what we read in Scripture. A study of the meaning of names is particularly interesting. In the Old Testament there is a very short four-chapter book called Ruth that is chock full of Bible gems. A most fascinating gem can be found in the names featured Ruth's first chapter. Ruth 1:1 starts out the account saying, *"Now it came to pass in the days when the judges ruled, that there was a famine in the land. And a certain man of Bethlehemjudah went to sojourn in the country of Moab, he, and his wife, and his two sons."* The book begins with a man named Elimelech who moved his family from Bethlehem in Judah to the country of Moab to avoid a famine. The meaning of their names combined with the actions and events of the first part of the story is where we find our Bible Gem today. Elimelech started out in the town of Bethlehem. The meaning of this town's name is the *"House of Bread."* This is a place named for God's provision. What is unusual about this name is that there was now a famine in this *"House of Bread."* How is this possible? It is because in the days of the Judges, Israel frequently turned their back on God. In Deuteronomy 28:15, 23 Israel was warned by God, *"[15]But it shall come to pass, if thou wilt not hearken unto the voice of the LORD thy God, to observe to do all his commandments and his statutes which I command thee this day; that all these curses shall come upon thee, and overtake thee...* [23] *And thy heaven that is over thy head shall be brass, and the earth that is under thee shall be iron."* The famine was the result of God's chastisement for their disobedience. So Elimelech, whose name means *"God is King"* has removed his family from the place of God's provision to go into the world as represented by Moab. In verse 2 we are introduced to the rest of the family. It reads, *"And the name of the man was Elimelech, and the name of his wife Naomi, and the name of his two sons Mahlon and Chilion, Ephrathites of Bethlehemjudah. And they came into the country of Moab, and continued there."* We are told that Elimelech's wife's name is Naomi, which means *"Pleasure,"* and they have two boys named Mahlon, which means *"Sickly,"* and Chilion, meaning *"Wasting Away."* So, we have *"God is King"* has married *"Pleasure"* and produce two children, *"Sickly"* and *"Wasting Away."* The lesson here is that when the church, who names Christ as King becomes enamored with pleasure, it produces Christians who are sickly and wasting away. A great percentage of churches today have sought a style of worship that elevates a pleasing emotional experience at the expense of remaining true to the Scriptures and magnifying the name of Christ. The result is the shallow Christianity we frequently find in America today. I hope that you desire something better than that in your life and your church today. I hope that you are willing to love God and His Word supremely and put off the desire for worldly pleasures.

# 6 – First Love

In Revelation chapter two we find the letter our Lord dictated to the Apostle John that was to be sent to the church at Ephesus. In verses 1-3, the Lord says, "*¹Unto the angel of the church of Ephesus write; These things saith he that holdeth the seven stars in his right hand, who walketh in the midst of the seven golden candlesticks; ²I know thy works, and thy labour, and thy patience, and how thou canst not bear them which are evil: and thou hast tried them which say they are apostles, and are not, and hast found them liars: ³And hast borne, and hast patience, and for my name's sake hast laboured, and hast not fainted.*" So, we have here a church that was "*doing*" everything right, held the right standards, and was busy for the Lord. In verse 4, however, the Lord says, "*Nevertheless I have somewhat against thee, because thou hast left thy first love.*" Though this church was doing right, their heart was not right and therefore, they were not right with the Lord. They had replaced spirituality with actions and standards. The Lord equates this to infidelity in a relationship because they left their "*first love.*" This Bible Gem stands as a warning to us that we cannot allow our motivation in serving the Lord to become a mere routine that leaves out a true love for our Lord. I heard a preacher once ask the rhetorical question, "*If the Holy Spirit left our churches, would our programs still go on?*" Doing the work of Christ without the power of Christ and a love for Him is of no value either here or in eternity. Fortunately, the Lord gives us the remedy for this problem in verse 5. *"Remember therefore from whence thou art fallen, and repent, and do the first works; or else I will come unto thee quickly, and will remove thy candlestick out of his place, except thou repent."* What is required when we find ourselves in this situation is to repent of our hardness of heart and fall in love with the Lord again. When a person first falls in love with the one they marry, the other person is almost constantly in their thoughts and heart. We need to feel that way towards the Lord that bought us with His precious blood. We ought to love Him and seek to be close to Him, not only on Sunday, but every day. Always desire to hear from Him and put His will above our own. Finally, do not do it because of His warning, but do it because we love Him and truly want to please Him! Remember 1 John 4:19, *"We love him, because he first loved us."* If we truly understand what the Lord has saved us from and the awful price He paid for our salvation, we almost cannot help but love Him!

Curious Puffin. Alaska Sea Life Center, Seward, Alaska, July 2012

# 7 – Rhoda Came to Hearken

Some people think that God has no sense of humor, but I totally disagree! In Acts chapter 12, we have a dire situation. Peter had been arrested and was awaiting execution by King Herod. The church had spent a sleepless night in prayer for Peter in the hope that God would allow him to somehow escape his fate. Their expectation was that during the night, as a result of their prayers, Herod would have a change of heart and decide to release Peter saying it was all a big mistake. That is not how God works most of the time. If that were the result, people might have said it was just coincidence. God was going to make sure there was no mistaking that He was the One who released Peter! The church at that time had forgotten the truth that would later be expressed in Ephesians 3:20. *"Now unto him that is able to do exceeding abundantly above all that we ask or think, according to the power that worketh in us,"* In answering prayer, God can and frequently does *"do exceeding abundantly above all that we ask or think!"* In this case, He exceeded their wildest expectations! God literally sent an angel to drag Peter out of his cell and yet the guards were completely unaware of the prison break! Peter, now having been left out in the street by the angel, goes to the house where the church was holding this prayer vigil. In Acts 12:13-14 we pick up the account. *"13And as Peter knocked at the door of the gate, a damsel came to hearken, named Rhoda. 14And when she knew Peter's voice, she opened not the gate for gladness, but ran in, and told how Peter stood before the gate.*" I consider this one of the funniest verses in Scripture! Rhoda was so excited that God had answered her prayer that she completely forgot to open the door! Poor Peter was still stuck out on the street waiting for the guards to notice his absence! God had done "*exceeding abundantly above all that*" she had asked or thought!

There are several gems in this short passage. We have already seen the gem that made us chuckle and the gem of how God exceeded what she had dreamed possible. There is, however, one other gem we can find as we continue on. In verses 16-17 we read, "*¹⁶But Peter continued knocking: and when they had opened the door, and saw him, they were astonished. ¹⁷But he, beckoning unto them with the hand to hold their peace, declared unto them how the Lord had brought him out of the prison. And he said, Go show these things unto James, and to the brethren. And he departed, and went into another place.*" After they finally let Peter in, they were astonished and excited about what had happened to him. Peter stopped their conversations so that he could declare what the Lord had done. The church was excited about Peter, but Peter wanted to make sure it was God that received the glory for what was done! Oh, that we would desire to do the same when God answers our prayers!

# 8 – A Burning Bush Experience

Recently my Pastor preached a message from Exodus chapter 3. He taught on how we each need to have a *"burning bush experience"* with the Lord. Chapter 3 begins with Moses tending the flocks of his father-in-law, Jethro, near Mt Horeb. Mount Horeb is the same mountain as Mount Sinai where the Ten Commandments would later be given. Moses spent the first forty years of his life in Egypt until he was forced to flee from Pharaoh for killing an Egyptian. He then spent forty years on the backside of the desert with Jethro's family. Moses was already a believer, having chosen the *"reproach of Christ"* over the riches of Egypt according to Hebrews 11:26. Now God was about to place a specific call on Moses; a call to lead Israel out of bondage in Egypt. Though we may never be called on to perform such a monumental task in our lives, God has something specific for each of us to do. In verses 2-4 we read, *"²And the angel of the LORD appeared unto him in a flame of fire out of the midst of a bush: and he looked, and, behold, the bush burned with fire, and the bush was not consumed. ³And Moses said, I will now turn aside, and see this great sight, why the bush is not burnt. ⁴And when the LORD saw that he turned aside to see, God called unto him out of the midst of the bush, and said, Moses, Moses. And he said, Here am I."* Moses observed the miracle, heard God call unto him, and willingly responded. We each should find a Bible Gem for ourselves in how God has dealt with us. In the hope that it will be an encouragement to you, I would like to share with you my burning bush experience that occurred a little over 2 years after I got saved.

When I was serving in the Air Force, I was deployed to the country of Turkey following the first Gulf War in the early 1990s. While there, I had the opportunity to take a boat trip in the Mediterranean. During that trip, we left the boat to swim over to some cliffs rising out of the water. No one realized it from the boat, but the waves were rough with about 3 feet between the top of the wave and the bottom of the trough. This made it extremely difficult to climb up the sheer cliff. The water was about 60 feet deep at the cliff face. I had to wait my turn to try to climb out. When my turn came, I grabbed hold of the rocks in the cliff. At the same moment the wave went out, ripping me from the rocks and dropping me straight down. Then the wave came back in and suddenly I was about three feet under the water. On top of that, there was an undertow there and I was caught in it! I struggled to get to the surface but could not. I eventually began swallowing seawater and was near to losing consciousness when the Lord brought to mind something I had heard preached in church. The preacher spoke about drowning in the sea of sin and reaching out to Jesus and He would save you. Though this was not the meaning of the preacher's message, I felt that the Lord was telling me to stop struggling and to reach out. I trusted Him and did so. Apparently, my hand broke the surface of the water, and someone grabbed hold of it. That was enough for me to begin climbing out and I scrambled up the rocks coughing up salt water as I went. I climbed up to a small ledge where everyone from the trip was sitting to catch their breath. It was there as I looked out over the beautiful Mediterranean that the Lord again spoke to me saying, *"I just saved your life, what are you going to do with it for Me?"* "Whatever you want, Lord," is how I replied. I have sought to serve Him faithfully ever since!

Not everyone will have so dramatic a *"burning bush experience,"* but the truth is that God has something for each of us to do. He wants you to stop and listen to what He has for you. Choose to be like Moses and turn aside to hear what the Lord is telling you today!

The actual cliffs where I nearly drowned. Alanya, Turkey, July 1994

# 9 – Touch of Compassion

A very special Bible Gem that reveals the depth of Christ's love for mankind is found in Matthew Chapter 8. As we read through the Gospel of Matthew, we find that our Lord's fame had spread throughout the land by the time this passage takes place. In Matthew 8:1-3 the Lord heals a leper that came to Him. The manner in which He does so, however, uniquely demonstrates His compassion for those in need. Here we read, *"¹When he was come down from the mountain, great multitudes followed him. ²And, behold, there came a leper and worshipped him, saying, Lord, if thou wilt, thou canst make me clean. ³And Jesus put forth his hand, and touched him, saying, I will; be thou clean. And immediately his leprosy was cleansed."* Did you see what was so special? It may help to try to visualize what is happening here. A great crowd had gathered, and a leper began to approach the crowd to see Jesus. The law required the leper to cry out *"unclean"* so that people could avoid touching him thus risking infecting themselves with the dreaded disease. As he approached the crowd, they would have parted like the Red Sea to avoid coming into contact with the leper. This made a path straight to our Lord. He then came to Christ and made his plea, *"Lord, if thou wilt, thou canst make me clean."* Keep in mind, that this man likely had not felt the touch of another human being in years, perhaps decades! The Lord's response to him is incredible. The Lord Jesus had proven before that He had the power to heal any condition to include leprosy with just a word, but that is not what He does here! Verse 3 says that "...*Jesus put forth his hand, and touched him, saying, I will; be thou clean...*" Not only did the Lord cleanse him from his leprosy, but also met the next greatest need he had. That need was for the touch of compassion which he received from none other than the Lord Jesus Christ. Oh, how unsearchable is the love of God?! How poor is our love for others compared to His great love?! We can barely stand to be around those we consider unlovely, or dirty, or unhealthy. We need to realize that every human being no matter how lowly or miserable is a soul for whom Jesus died! They are souls that will spend eternity in either Heaven or Hell! We too need to have compassion for them and seek to bring them to the Saviour! David, when fleeing from King Saul, said in Psalm 142:4, "*I looked on my right hand, and beheld, but there was no man that would know me: refuge failed me; no man cared for my soul.*"—People are lost and dying and going to Hell—We must care!!!

Corral in Monument Valley, Arizona, July 2007

# 10 – The Blood of These Men

As a retired military man, I appreciate the biblical record of Israel in combat. In 2 Samuel 23:14-17 we have a record of one of King David's many battles. Verse 14 tells us, "*And David was then in a hold, and the garrison of the Philistines was then in Bethlehem.*" Israel was fighting against the Philistines for possession of David's hometown of Bethlehem. The Philistines had taken over the town and David was fighting to take it back. As David looked over the battlefield, he was overcome with nostalgia for his birthplace and makes an off-handed comment that he probably did not intend anyone to hear. Verse 15 says, "*And David longed, and said, Oh that one would give me drink of the water of the well of Bethlehem, which is by the gate!*" The comment, however, did not fall on deaf ears! His three mighty men heard and responded to their king's wish. Verses 16 and 17, complete the story of this exploit, "*[16]And the three mighty men broke through the host of the Philistines, and drew water out of the well of Bethlehem, that was by the gate, and took it, and brought it to David: nevertheless he would not drink thereof, but poured it out unto the LORD. [17]And he said, Be it far from me, O LORD, that I should do this: is not this the blood of the men that went in jeopardy of their lives? therefore he would not drink it. These things did these three mighty men.*"

This was an amazing military feat! The three mighty men disregarded the danger to their lives to fulfill the king's slightest desire. Pleasing the king was all that mattered. In so doing, it must have also struck fear in the hearts of the enemy. The lack of regard for the enemy's military strength when they broke through the lines for something as seemingly trivial as a cup of water, must certainly have made them doubt their ability to stand against Israel. The risk and sacrifice did not go unappreciated by David either. He refused to drink their offering, having understood that only the Lord deserves such devotion!

Pray that we would have such devotion to the things of God that we would instantly respond to anything the Lord gives us to do. Whether it be an opportunity to be a witness, or to help the Lord's work financially, or to give of our time and our gifts, we need to be instant in our service and devotion to the Lord. When we do, God, like David in this passage, will not fail to recognize our efforts. Hebrews 6:10 reminds us, *"For God is not unrighteous to forget your work and labor of love, which ye have showed toward his name, in that ye have ministered to the saints, and do minister."*

# 11 – Absolute Surrender

Are you surrendered to the will of God in all areas of your life? In Luke 9:23-24, our Lord Jesus speaks to us regarding this matter. The verses read, *"²³And he said to them all, If any man will come after me, let him deny himself, and take up his cross daily, and follow me. ²⁴For whosoever will save his life shall lose it: but whosoever will lose his life for my sake, the same shall save it."* We need to be constantly devoted to our Lord. Christianity is not just something for Sunday morning but is, rather, a complete way of life that begins with salvation. Sadly, many people who profess to know Christ are satisfied with much less in their life. The 19ᵗʰ century (1828-1917) Christian author, Andrew Murray, said in his book, Absolute Surrender (p. 8), *"But once, in Scotland, I was in a company where we talked about the condition of Christ's Church, and what the great need of the Church and of believers is. There was in our company a godly Christian worker who has much to do in training other workers for Christ, and I asked him what he would say was the great need of the Church—the message that ought to be preached. He answered very quietly and simply and determinedly: 'Absolute surrender to God is the one thing.'"* The author goes on, *"The words struck me as never before. And that man began to tell how, in the Christian workers with whom he had to deal, he finds that if they are sound on that point, they are willing to be taught and helped, and they always improve. Whereas, others who are not sound there very often go back and leave the work. The condition for obtaining God's full blessing is absolute surrender to Him."* Nothing has changed since those words were written. The great need in believers today is still for absolute surrender to God. The Lord said as much to us when He said, *"If any man will come after me, let him deny himself, and take up his cross daily, and follow me."* In order to truly please God and to fulfill our purpose here on earth requires the submission of our will to that of God! Each day we must set aside our lives and take up the cross of Christ. In Galatians 2:20 the apostle Paul tells us, *"I am crucified with Christ: nevertheless I live; yet not I, but Christ liveth in me: and the life which I now live in the flesh I live by the faith of the Son of God, who loved me, and gave himself for me."* Let us be absolutely surrendered to God in our daily lives so that when this life is over, we can enter into God's presence and hear Him say, *"Well done, thou good and faithful servant!"*

Sunset over the Mediterranean Sea, Tel Aviv, Israel, June 2007

# 12 – Saddest Verse

Today's Bible Gem is what I consider one of the saddest verses in all of Scripture. In Deuteronomy chapter 5, Moses was nearing the end of his ministry and was taking the opportunity to remind the people of when they first received the Ten Commandments from God. This occurred when Israel first arrived at Mount Sinai, before Moses went to receive the stone tablets written with the finger of God. The people were gathered at the base of the mountain and physically heard God speak as He verbally gave them the Commandments. In verse 24, Moses reminds them of what they said in their surprise at having heard God speak. "*And ye said, Behold, the LORD our God hath shewed us his glory and his greatness, and we have heard his voice out of the midst of the fire: we have seen this day that God doth talk with man, and he liveth.*" They were amazed that they could hear the most holy God speak and not have been struck dead for it! But in the very next verse the people say, "*Now therefore why should we die? for this great fire will consume us: if we hear the voice of the LORD our God any more, then we shall die.*" The people then asked Moses to be the only one that would speak with God and to relay those messages to them so that they could obey Him. How odd that after hearing God once they now somehow feared He would destroy them. The reason for this is fairly simple. God had expressed His Law to them but after examining their own lives, they realized all the ways they had failed to meet His requirements. Not only that, but they were unwilling to change their lives to live by His Law and therefore were in danger of God's wrath. In verse 28, the Lord tells Moses that the people's fears were well founded, but in verse 29 we can almost hear God's heart break. He says to Moses, *"O that there were such an heart in them, that they would fear me, and keep all my commandments always, that it might be well with them, and with their children for ever!"* God was saying that if Israel would only do what He said, everything would be fine. His heart was breaking because He knew they would not do it and were He to continue to speak directly to them, He would have to judge them and destroy them. Why? Because they would not deal with their sin! Like Israel of old, I believe America is breaking God's heart today. We love our sin and have lost our craving for a closeness with God. To have that requires that we deal with our sin and that is a greater price than we want to pay. We love the world more than we love God and we have broken His heart. All that is left to us is judgement unless we repent and turn back to God. Oh, that we would have a heart for God. Oh, that we would fear Him and keep His commandments…not as a means of salvation, but for those who are saved, as a means of pleasing our Savior. Let us turn from the worldly lusts of the flesh and preach the Gospel to this lost and dying world that others may be saved and learn how to please God as well! *"O that there were such an heart in them, that they would fear me, and keep all my commandments always, that it might be well with them, and with their children for ever!"*

# 13 – The Mind of Christ

Today's Bible Gem is found in Philippians 2:5 where we are encouraged to have the mind of Christ. It reads, *"Let this mind be in you, which was also in Christ Jesus:"* ...but what is the mind of Christ that we are commanded to have? The entire passage of Philippians 2:5-8 sheds light on this. *"⁵Let this mind be in you, which was also in Christ Jesus: ⁶Who, being in the form of God, thought it not robbery to be equal with God: ⁷But made himself of no reputation, and took upon him the form of a servant, and was made in the likeness of men: ⁸And being found in fashion as a man, he humbled himself, and became obedient unto death, even the death of the cross."*

So, what is the mind of Christ? First, the mind of Christ is—Humility. Verse 8 tells us of the Lord Jesus that *"...he humbled himself..."* (vs. 8). Truly the Lord Jesus was the humblest person to ever walk the face of the earth. He was and is God, the Creator of the heavens and earth, and yet He took on human flesh and lived among us. Not only that, but He then tasted death to save us from sin. Verse 8, *"And being found in fashion as a man, he humbled himself, and became obedient unto death, even the death of the cross."* Since we are to have the mind of Christ, that means we are commanded to demonstrate humility. In verse 3 of this passage we are told, *"Let nothing be done through strife or vainglory; but in lowliness of mind let each esteem other better than themselves."*

Next, the mind of Christ is—Love. In verse 7 we are told that the Lord "...*was made in the likeness of men.*" Why would the Lord of Glory do that? Love! John 3:16 tells the reason the Lord Jesus came to this world. "*For God so loved the world, that he gave his only begotten Son, that whosoever believeth in him should not perish, but have everlasting life.*" It was love that drove Christ to the cross. We too are commanded by God to love. In 1 John 4:8 we are told, "*He that loveth not knoweth not God; for God is love.*" Frankly, if you have not learned to love one another, you have not learned to please God. In fact, the Lord said that love was the one thing that would make us stand out from the world as his followers. In John 13:34-35, the Lord Jesus says, "*34A new commandment I give unto you, That ye love one another; as I have loved you, that ye also love one another. 35By this shall all men know that ye are my disciples, if ye have love one to another.*"

Finally, the mind of Christ is—Obedience. Verse 8 tells us "*...he humbled himself, and became obedient unto death, even the death of the cross.*" The Lord Jesus tells us that He came to this earth out of obedience to the Father's will. John 6:38, "For I came down from heaven, not to do mine own will, but the will of him that sent me." To have the mind of Christ requires us to be obedient to God's will as He has revealed it to us in His Word. We must not resist God's will but should seek to obey Him in all things. Verses 13-14 reminds us, "*13For it is God which worketh in you both to will and to do of his good pleasure. 14Do all* *things without murmurings and disputings:*" We need to obey God without complaining and grumbling as we often do. In America today we are obsessed with self, but God's way is for us to die to ourselves and live for Him. Matthew 16:24-25 says, "*[24]Then said Jesus unto his disciples, If any man will come after me, let him deny himself, and take up his cross, and follow me. [25]For whosoever will save his life shall lose it: and whosoever will lose his life for my sake shall find it.*"

We are commanded to have the mind of Christ. From Scripture, the mind of Christ is humility, the mind of Christ is love, and the mind of Christ is obedience. "*Let this mind be in you, which was also in Christ Jesus:*"

Keukenhof Gardens, Holland, April 2005

# 14 – Purpose of Heart

For the most part, we all know the story of Daniel in the Lions' Den, but we often do not think about what brought Daniel to the place in life where he was both cast into the lions or how through his faith, God delivered him. In case someone may not know, Daniel was among the Jews taken captive in Babylon and had risen to prominence in the Persian Empire that ruled the region at that time. The other rulers of the land, who were pagans, resented Daniel and wanted to accuse him of wrongdoing so that he might be killed. Daniel 6:4-5, however, tells us that they could find nothing to accuse Daniel of apart from worshipping God! The verses say, "*⁴Then the presidents and princes sought to find occasion against Daniel concerning the kingdom; but they could find none occasion nor fault; forasmuch as he was faithful, neither was there any error or fault found in him.  ⁵Then said these men, We shall not find any occasion against this Daniel, except we find it against him concerning the law of his God.*" Ultimately, they managed to get a law passed to make it illegal for anyone to pray to any god or person other than the king. This, of course, did not keep Daniel from praying to God, as always, and as a punishment he was cast into the lions' den intending that he would be killed immediately. The next morning, Daniel emerged from the lions' den without a mark on him. He declared in verse 22, "*My God hath sent his angel, and hath shut the lions' mouths, that they have not hurt me: forasmuch as before him innocency was found in me; and also before thee, O king, have I done no hurt."* Daniel's accusers were then cast to the lions and were consumed without delay.

At that time in Daniel's life, he was over 80 years old. When these wicked men wanted to accuse him of doing wrong, the only thing they could accuse him of was serving the Lord. The fact that God preserved Daniel's life through the night also attests to his faithfulness. That is not to say that Daniel was entirely without sin because the bible is clear in Romans 3:23, *"For all have sinned, and come short of the glory of God."* But the Bible also attests to his faithfulness and generally righteous life. How could a man live such a long life of faithfulness? The answer lies in Daniel chapter 1. When Daniel was taken captive in Babylon, he was only a teenager. At that time, he made a conscious decision. Daniel 1:8 tells us, *"But Daniel purposed in his heart that **he would not defile himself** with the portion of the king's meat, nor with the wine which he drank: therefore he requested of the prince of the eunuchs that he might not defile himself."* At this young age, Daniel *"purposed in his heart"* to be faithful to God and then lived his whole life with that purpose in mind. We too need to purpose in our hearts to be faithful to God. It is best to decide this when you are young, like Daniel, so that you can live your whole life serving Him. Failing that, it is still not too late to make that decision and begin to be faithful. As long as you have breath it is worth living the rest of your life for the Lord! Daniel's life is a true Bible Gem that proves it is possible to be faithful throughout one's life and that is what we should aspire to do!

A Lonely Road, Yukon, Canada, May 2012

# 15 – Taste and See!

Back in the 1980s, while I was in the Air Force stationed at Castle AFB in CA, a friend of mine that served with me told me of his favorite hamburger place. He was from Los Angeles. He insisted that In-n-Out Burger was the best hamburger place in the country. He told me about these burgers repeatedly until one day I had the opportunity to try one. I personally do not get overly excited about food, but I had to admit, it was good! Now any time I am in the southwest I try to stop at an In-n-Out Burger. At first, I had heard how good this food was, but it was not until I had tasted it that I truly knew how good it was.

In Psalm 34, the psalmist, David, had fled from King Saul only to try and hide among Israel's great enemy the Philistines. This turned out to be a terrible place to hide because the Philistines had already suffered many defeats at the hands of David. David narrowly escaped death at the hands of King Abimelech by feigning insanity. In this Psalm, David was thanking God for preserving his life in that situation and for His goodness to him in general. In verse 8, David exhorts us, *"O taste and see that the LORD is good: blessed is the man that trusteth in him."* You may have heard that God is good. You may even believe that He is, but have you truly tasted His goodness? Believers in Christ have tasted of His goodness, and we love to tell others of Him. Until you have experienced His deliverance out of trials and temptations or His presence in times of trouble and testing, you have not "*tasted*" of His goodness. Proverbs 18:24 describes Him as "*a friend that sticketh closer than a brother.*" In Psalm 46:1, "*God is our refuge and strength, a very present help in trouble.*" God provides for our needs, protects us, and freely gives us His infinite love. We know of the sufferings of Job and the trials he faced. At the end of those trials, Job conversed with God and realized just how great and good He truly is. In Job 42:5, Job exclaims to God, "*I have heard of thee by the hearing of the ear: but now mine eye seeth thee.*"

Have you tasted of God's goodness today? You can if you trust in Christ as your Saviour. This wicked world and the sins we are all guilty of will leave a bitter taste, but the sweetness of our Lord can wipe that away forever. Acts 16:31 tells us, "*...Believe on the Lord Jesus Christ, and thou shalt be saved...*" Today if you will repent of your sin and call upon Jesus Christ to save you, believing that He died on the cross for your sins, you will be saved and can taste of God's goodness. Romans 10:13 tells us, "*For whosoever shall call upon the name of the Lord shall be saved.*" Please trust in Jesus Christ today and if you do, please give us a call so we can help you find a good church and begin your new life in Christ. You can give us a call at 502-531-0534 or send us a quick email at wiopfmradio@gmail.com. "*O taste and see that the LORD is good...*"

# 16 – What Doth the Lord Require?

What does the Lord expect from you as a Christian? That is an important question and is brought to us in Micah 6:8 where the answer is found. The prophet says, *"He hath shewed thee, O man, what is good; and what doth the LORD require of thee, but to do justly, and to love mercy, and to walk humbly with thy God?"* This gem has three facets that show us exactly what the Lord requires of His children. Mind you, these are His requirements for those who are already believers and have been saved by the precious blood of the Lord Jesus. Good works cannot save you. Only faith in Jesus Christ can do that. For believers, however, these things are what God expects of us that we may be right with Him.

The first thing God requires is *"to do justly."* The verse reminds us that God has *"shewed thee, O man, what is good."* He has done this in His Word. We are commanded in 1 Peter 1:16, *"Be ye holy; for I am holy."* How holy is God? How much holiness do we settle for? In Romans 12:1-2 we are told to be a living sacrifice. This means we cannot live for ourselves, fulfilling our own desires, but must live for God always.

Second, we are *"to love mercy."* As God has had mercy on us, we are to forgive others and demonstrate love regardless of whether that love is returned or not. In Matthew 18:21-22, the Lord talks to Peter about forgiveness. *"²¹Then came Peter to him, and said, Lord, how oft shall my brother sin against me, and I forgive him? till seven times?* $^{22}$*Jesus saith unto him, I say not unto thee, Until seven times: but, Until seventy times seven."* Mercy is a demonstration of unconditional love. In John 13:35 the Lord instructs us, *"By this shall all men know that ye are my disciples, if ye have love one to another."*

The third thing the Lord requires is "*...to walk humbly with thy God...*" In James 4:6 we read, *"But he giveth more grace. Wherefore he saith, God resisteth the proud, but giveth grace unto the humble."* True humility is not self-hatred or blaming oneself for everything, but simply a recognition of our own unworthiness and our complete dependence upon God. Titus 3:5 reminds us that we are only sinners saved by the grace of God. *"Not by works of righteousness which we have done, but according to his mercy he saved us, by the washing of regeneration, and renewing of the Holy Ghost;"* We can neither save ourselves nor live a life pleasing to God without His grace.

The question is asked here, *"what doth the LORD require of thee?"* The prophet answers his own question and shows us how to live for God. *"He hath shewed thee, O man, what is good; and what doth the LORD require of thee, but to do justly, and to love mercy, and to walk humbly with thy God?"*

Humpback Whale, Seward, Alaska, May 2012

# 17 – Coming Again

Of all the Bible Gems we have considered so far, this has to be one of the diamonds! In Acts chapter 1, the risen Lord Jesus gives some final instructions to His Disciples before He ascends into Heaven. In verse 8 He says, *"But ye shall receive power, after that the Holy Ghost is come upon you: and ye shall be witnesses unto me both in Jerusalem, and in all Judaea, and in Samaria, and unto the uttermost part of the earth."* Following these words, He then ascended into the air where a cloud received Him from their sight. They stood staring in amazement until two angels appeared and spoke to them. Acts 1:10-11 tells us, *"[10]And while they looked stedfastly toward heaven as he went up, behold, two men stood by them in white apparel; [11]Which also said, Ye men of Galilee, why stand ye gazing up into heaven? this same Jesus, which is taken up from you into heaven, shall so come in like manner as ye have seen him go into heaven."* Jesus is coming again! The angels said, "this same Jesus," not a substitute or a representative. This same Jesus that shed His precious blood for our sins is coming again! This same Jesus that rose from the dead after three days in the grave is coming again! This same Jesus who said in John 14:3, *"And if I go and prepare a place for you, I will come again, and receive you unto myself; that where I am, there ye may be also."* is coming again!!! Jesus is coming again…and perhaps very soon! Today many scoff at this truth and mock those who believe His promise! 2 Peter 3:3-4 points out that this is one of the signs of the end. *"³Knowing this first, that there shall come in the last days scoffers, walking after their own lusts, ⁴And saying, Where is the promise of his coming? for since the fathers fell asleep, all things continue as they were from the beginning of the creation."* Though they may scoff and mock, the truth is that Christ is coming again, just as He promised! Our Lord's last recorded words in Revelation 22:20 are, *"Surely I come quickly."* To which the Apostle John replies, *"Amen. Even so, come, Lord Jesus."* For those who truly know Jesus Christ as their personal Saviour, we have His precious promise that He will come soon to remove His church from this wicked and hateful world. As we see the world around us descending into chaos, we can know that that day is approaching quickly! We should rejoice with John and exclaim, *"Come, Lord Jesus!"*

Mentasta Lake, Alaska, May 2012

# 18 – God's Missionary

A missionary can be defined as a person commissioned to go to a foreign field with a message of faith. Therefore, to be a missionary, one must have a right Field, a right Commission, and a right Message. With this definition in mind, we must consider the Lord Jesus Christ to be the greatest missionary who ever walked the face of the earth! In John 3:16 we read *"For God so loved the world, that he gave his only begotten Son, that whosoever believeth in him should not perish, but have everlasting life."* He was sent to the greatest field, by the greatest commission, with the greatest message!

First, the Lord Jesus was sent to the greatest field (*"For God so loved the world..."*)! That field was to every nation of this entire world! He came to reach this lost and dying human race before it was eternally too late. Galatians 4:4-5, *"⁴But when the fulness of the time was come, God sent forth his Son, made of a woman, made under the law, ⁵To redeem them that were under the law, that we might receive the adoption of sons."* Our Lord left the glories of Heaven on a mission to save lost mankind in every nation.

Next, our Lord Jesus was sent by the greatest commission (*"...that he gave his only begotten Son..."*)! The Lord Jesus Christ was sent on His mission to save us by God, the Father. In John 6:38-39, the Lord Jesus tells us, *"³⁸For I came down from heaven, not to do mine own will, but the will of him that sent me. ³⁹And this is the Father's will which hath sent me, that of all which he hath given me I should lose nothing, but should raise it up again at the last day.*" The Son of God came to us as He was bidden of the Father…to die for our sins and redeem us to Himself.

Finally, the Lord Jesus was sent with the greatest message ever heard ("*…that whosoever believeth in him should not perish, but have everlasting life.*")! There is only one message and only one salvation from sin! In Acts 4:12 we read, "*Neither is there salvation in any other: for there is none other name under heaven given among men, whereby we must be saved.*" If we reject His message, there is no other hope! Hebrews 2:3 asks us, "*How shall we escape, if we neglect so great salvation; which at the first began to be spoken by the Lord, and was confirmed unto us by them that heard him;*"

Have you responded to the Lord's message of salvation? In Acts 16:31 we read, "*Believe on the Lord Jesus Christ, and thou shalt be saved…*" The Lord Jesus was sent by the Father to this earth to die for your sins. Won't you repent of your sin and believe on the Lord Jesus Christ as your Saviour today? If you are saved, won't you follow our Lord's example and become a missionary right here at home by getting the Gospel out to the lost and dying world that is around you every day! The Lord has given us that mission and we need to be busy about that work in this world!

# 19 – The Peace of God

One thing people seem to lack in this world is genuine peace. Life is frequently a series of struggles and setbacks. Depression is the true pandemic that plagues our world. In 2017, the World Health Organization listed depression as the leading cause of disability in the world (United Nations, 2017). People around the globe are living in despair, but it need not be so! In Philippians 4:6-7, we are encouraged to "*⁶Be careful for nothing; but in every thing by prayer and supplication with thanksgiving let your requests be made known unto God. ⁷And the peace of God, which passeth all understanding, shall keep your hearts and minds through Christ Jesus.*"

These verses admonish us to be careful…that is to be full of care and worry…for nothing. We need not be anxious or worried because we are always in God's hands. Whether things go right or wrong, we are to bring them before the Lord in prayer. When we do that with humility and thanksgiving, we have a promise of the peace of God which the world cannot understand! This is truly a Bible gem of great value. Whatever we face in this life, we can rest in the knowledge that God is still in control and watching over us. When we realize this, we can begin to experience His peace that passeth understanding!

We are reminded of this in the words of the song Constantly Abiding.

*"There's a peace in my heart that the world never gave,*
*A peace it cannot take away;*
*Though the trials of life may surround like a cloud,*
*I've a peace that has come here to stay!"*

As dark as this world may become, we can rest on our Saviour's words in John 14:27. *"Peace I leave with you, my peace I give unto you: not as the world giveth, give I unto you. Let not your heart be troubled, neither let it be afraid."* When this world gets you down and you begin to despair, turn to the Lord in prayer and He will give you that peace that passeth understanding! When the storms of life feel like they will overwhelm your soul, remember, it is the Lord who calms the tempests, and it is the Lord who walks through them with us. If you know Christ as your Saviour, you can have that peace and let Him keep your heart and mind through the trails of life.

White Peacock in the Tulips, Keukenhof Gardens, Holland, April 2005

# 20 – Exceeding Abundantly Above

Ephesians 3:20-21 tells us, "*[20]Now unto him that is able to do exceeding abundantly above all that we ask or think, according to the power that worketh in us, [21]Unto him be glory in the church by Christ Jesus throughout all ages, world without end. Amen.*" The Lord is described as being able to do "*exceeding abundantly above all that we ask or think.*" There is literally nothing too hard for God to do! The greatest hindrance to our prayers is not God's ability to answer them, it is our unbelief. Yet this is something we all struggle with by nature. As finite created beings, the true power and ability of God is something beyond our comprehension. In Mark 9:24 we read of the father of a demoniac child, "*And straightway the father of the child cried out, and said with tears, Lord, I believe; help thou mine unbelief.*" Though he knew the Lord could do what he asked for his child, he still struggled with believing it and asked the Lord to help him with even that.

We often pray for things but in the back of our mind we think that God will not answer this prayer because "*He just doesn't work that way.*" We limit God through our unbelief. This thought was brought home to me many years ago while I was stationed in England in the military. I had taken some time off so I could drive up to Scotland. Before leaving on the trip, I checked the oil in the car. It was low so I added a quart of oil and headed out on the road. We drove up into Scotland and then the following day drove up into the highlands. On the way back to the place we were staying at, I noticed smoke coming up from the engine and smelled a burning odor. At that very moment we *"just happened"* to come to a gas station, so I stopped. The road we were travelling was well away from any town, so the presence of the gas station was by God's providence as well. We pulled in and I popped open the hood of the car. Apparently when I put oil in the car, I had failed to put the filler cap back on and all the oil from the engine had sprayed over the engine compartment and was *"cooking"* from the heat being produced. I had left the filler cap on top of the engine, but now it was nowhere to be seen. I went into the gas station and purchased some oil and filled the reservoir. I walked back in to ask if they had a cap that would fit my car and they replied, *"No, mate. We don't have anything like that."* Walking back to the car I began to pray. The exact words I prayed were, *"Lord, I know it is virtually impossible and that you don't work this way, but would you please allow me to find the oil cap somewhere."* I began looking around the area on top of the engine where I had left it and, of course, it was not there. I started looking lower down until I came to where the axle for the left front wheel was. There was a little ledge there and I found the cap just sitting there. Using a wrench to extend my reach I tapped it, and it fell straight to the ground...nothing was holding it there. We had driven over 900 miles on the motorways of England and on the mountain roads of Scotland for two days and it had never fallen off. I am convinced an angel had been flying along next to us with his hand on the cap saying, *"will you please stop?!"*

The reality is that God had answered my prayer despite my unbelief as a way of getting me to trust Him more. I was humbled and ashamed of my doubt, but I had learned that God does truly do *"exceeding abundantly above all that we ask or think."* He can do the same for you. If you are a child of God, pray according to His will and He will exceed your expectations and meet the needs of your life as well.

Cliffs near Tintagel Castle, England, July 2019

# 21 – Wake Up!

Good morning church! This is your wakeup call from God! Today's Bible gem comes from Romans 13 verses 11-14, "*[11]And that, knowing the time, that now it is high time to awake out of sleep: for now is our salvation nearer than when we believed. [12]The night is far spent, the day is at hand: let us therefore cast off the works of darkness, and let us put on the armour of light. [13]Let us walk honestly, as in the day; not in rioting and drunkenness, not in chambering and wantonness, not in strife and envying. [14]But put ye on the Lord Jesus Christ, and make not provision for the flesh, to fulfil the lusts thereof.*" We live in a time when the world is moving further and further from God every day. It seems like everything is spiraling out of control. To begin with, we need to understand that God is still, and always will be, in control. However, our passage today reminds us that our time is short on this Earth. "*The night is far spent, the day is at hand.*" Christ is coming soon, and we must be busy for Him. Unfortunately, the church as a whole seems to be asleep on duty. The average believer today is far more focused on the affairs of this world and spends minimal time in prayer, and in the Bible. We are more concerned with what's on Netflix than we are with what we've been reading in the Word. Our next promotion at work occupies our thoughts far more than the things of God. Spiritually we are asleep. Scripture admonishes us that it is high time to awake out of sleep. As we look at the signs of the times, we can see that the night is indeed far spent. We need to wake up and get busy for the Lord. The song *"Turn Your Eyes upon Jesus"* (Lemmel, 1922) tells us that we are to look upon the Lord Jesus and that when we do *"the things of earth will grow strangely dim."* Their importance loses its value, as we see the value of Jesus Christ.

So, according to this passage, how do we wake up? *"Let us therefore cast off the works of darkness, and let us put on the armor of light."* We are caught up in this world's darkness and we must break free of it by living a separated and holy life for Jesus Christ. Wealth, success, and advancement in this world mean nothing in the light of eternity. The gold we so diligently seek here is worthy only of being used for paving material on the streets of Heaven. In the words of C.T. Studd (1884), *"Only one life, twill soon be past. Only what's done for Christ will last."* What matters is the people we reach for Christ, and the stand we take <u>against</u> the works of darkness and <u>for</u> the Lord. History is replete with examples of believers who laid down their lives for the Gospel's sake and yet we feel we have been persecuted if someone makes a rude comment towards us. We need to wake up and start living for Christ today. The Lord is coming again, and it may be very soon! Let's make our time here mean something. *"Now it is high time to awake out of sleep!"*

51

# 22 – Study the Word

2 Timothy 2:15 reads, *"Study to shew thyself approved unto God, a workman that needeth not to be ashamed, rightly dividing the word of truth."* We need to study the Bible!

*"A Barna poll indicated that at least 12 percent of adults believe that Joan of Arc was Noah's wife. Another survey of graduating high school seniors revealed that over 50 percent thought that Sodom and Gomorrah were husband and wife. A considerable number of respondents to one poll indicated that the Sermon on the Mount was preached by Billy Graham."* (Mohler, 2016)

We may laugh at these responses, but the truth is that biblical illiteracy in our world today has grown to epidemic proportions. It is sad, but people generally have little or no understanding of the Scriptures! Let this not be said of us! Our verse today says that if we want God's approval in our lives, we need to study His Word. God did not say soul winning was the key to His approval. Nor did He say prayer. Nor holy living. …But study! Why is that? Because studying and knowing God's Word compels one to win souls and pray and live holy. If His Word is the foundation, everything else falls into place. If we lose the Word of God as the foundation of our life, Psalm 11:3 warns us, *"If the foundations be destroyed, what can the righteous do?"* We need to be in the Bible every day and think on what we read throughout the whole day. Psalm

1:2 says of the man who is blessed of God, *"But his delight is in the law of the LORD; and in his law doth he meditate day and night."* Let us daily make the Word of God our delight and we will have a life that will please God. What you care about will define how you live. What you care about will govern what you speak of. What you care about will direct where you go. Let the Word of God be what we care about.

Our verse also says that study will make us an unashamed workman. There is much work to do in this Christian life. It is God's Word that directs us in that work. No one likes a coworker that does not do their job well because they create more work for everyone else on the job. To be the worker for the Lord that "needeth not to be ashamed," we must study and know God's Word. We must have the Word of God working in us, for us to work for Christ. 1 Thessalonians 2:13 tells us, *"For this cause also thank we God without ceasing, because, when ye received the word of God which ye heard of us, ye received it not as the word of men, but as it is in truth, the word of God, which effectually worketh also in you that believe."* It is the Word of God working in us and through us that we need in order to be the right workman.

Finally, it is through study that we learn to rightly divide the word of truth. We study throughout our Christian life to understand the Word better and to know God more! It is through these years of study that we learn sound doctrine. Ephesians 4:14, *"That we henceforth be no more children, tossed to and fro, and carried about with every wind of doctrine, by the sleight of men, and cunning craftiness, whereby they lie in wait to deceive;"* The immunization for being carried away by false doctrines is a good dose of the rightly divided Word of God!

*"Study to shew thyself approved unto God, a workman that needeth not to be ashamed, rightly dividing the word of truth."*

Synagogue of Capernaum, Israel, June 2007

# 23 – Be a Barnabas

I want to talk to you about Barnabas today. His name means "son of consolation." In Scripture we find that he was an encourager. In particular, he was an encouragement to Paul, the apostle. Paul was the spiritual giant of the first century. He wrote most of the books in the New Testament. However, without Barnabas, Paul might never have amounted to anything. Right after Paul got saved, he went to the church at Jerusalem. Those in Jerusalem had heard of this man, who was known as Saul at that time. He was the great persecutor of the church. In Acts 9:26 we read about his arrival at the church. *"And when Saul was come to Jerusalem, he assayed to join himself to the disciples: but they were all afraid of him, and believed not that he was a disciple."* At first Paul was not trusted by anyone in the church. Not by anyone, that is, except Barnabas. Acts 9:27 says, *"But Barnabas took him, and brought him to the apostles, and declared unto them how he had seen the Lord in the way, and that he had spoken to him, and how he had preached boldly at Damascus in the name of Jesus."* When Paul was rejected, Barnabas stepped in to help him begin his Christian life. Paul was seeking to serve the Lord and Barnabas was there to give him his chance. Paul begins preaching there in Jerusalem, but his former associates from when he persecuted the church, now sought to kill him. The disciples sent him back to his hometown of Tarsus for his own protection.

That might have been the last time we heard of Paul were it not for Barnabas! At this time, the Gentiles began to receive the gospel, and many were saved. This was mainly happening in Antioch, Syria. When word reached Jerusalem, they sent Barnabas to investigate. He found the reports were true. He took time to encourage those young believers and then went to seek someone who had been on his heart of late. He went to find Saul of Tarsus…Paul.

Acts 11:25 tells us, *"Then departed Barnabas to Tarsus, for to seek Saul:"* After leaving Jerusalem for Tarsus, Paul seems to have settled down into a nominal Christian life for a time. He was content to just serve the Lord in his hometown. Barnabas, however, saw greater potential in Paul and went to find him. Acts 11:26 tells us, *"And when he had found him, he brought him unto Antioch. And it came to pass, that a whole year they assembled themselves with the church, and taught much people. And the disciples were called Christians first in Antioch."* Barnabas brought Paul to the church in Antioch and helped him get involved. The two men then go on to become the first international missionaries sent from the church. We need to realize that without Barnabas we would not have had Paul and without Paul we would not have most of the New Testament nor the churches mentioned therein! In our Christian life, we may not have the ability to be a spiritual giant like Paul, but we can all be an encouragement to others in the work of the Lord. Be a Barnabas to someone today!

# 24 – Eyes on Eternity

We must have an eternal perspective in life! Our Bible Gem today comes from 2 Corinthians 4:18, *"While we look not at the things which are seen, but at the things which are not seen: for the things which are seen are temporal; but the things which are not seen are eternal."* We live in two worlds at the same time, one seen and one unseen. The spiritual world is an unseen world, and it is the one that we tend to overlook and forget each day. We focus on the physical world, but that is the less important and more transient of the two. We run around seeking this world's approval and riches, but those things are not eternal. 2 Peter 3:10 assures us, *"But the day of the Lord will come as a thief in the night; in the which the heavens shall pass away with a great noise, and the elements shall melt with fervent heat, the earth also and the works that are therein shall be burned up."* Even our earthly life is temporary. James 4:14 reminds us, *"Whereas ye know not what shall be on the morrow. For what is your life? It is even a vapour, that appeareth for a little time, and then vanisheth away."* In this world, our supreme duty is to serve the Lord. Nothing else truly matters in life. Simply trust God and follow His will. He will provide and lead and reward.

The spiritual world on the other hand is the true reality. 2 Corinthians 5:7, *"(For we walk by faith, not by sight:)"* The spiritual reality of this life is something that only the saved can clearly see. John 3:3, *"Jesus answered and said unto him, Verily, verily, I say unto thee, Except a man be born again, he cannot see the kingdom of God."* Oh, a lost person may perceive some spiritual forces, but those things are out of context and lead to deception. Only a born-again believer peering through the window of God's Word can correctly perceive the spiritual world. We must work for things eternal! C.T. Studd, a missionary around the year 1900, once wrote,

> *"Only one life, twill soon be past, Only what's done for Christ will last." We need to focus on those things that have eternal significance…the souls of others…the will of God…the preaching and teaching of the Word of God! In this world God is sifting out the saved and the lost. We need to be busy about reaching the lost while there is still time. God is also working in us to be conformed to the image of Christ. These are the things that matter for eternity and are part of the spiritual reality.*

Our struggle is a spiritual one. Ephesians 6:11-12, *"Put on the whole armour of God, that ye may be able to stand against the wiles of the devil. For we wrestle not against flesh and blood, but against principalities, against powers, against the rulers of the darkness of this world, against spiritual wickedness in high places."* The real reality and struggle in life is a spiritual one and we need to focus on that reality if we are to lead a life that pleases God.

# 25 – Looking unto Jesus

Today's Bible gem comes from Hebrews 12:1-3, *"¹Wherefore seeing we also are compassed about with so great a cloud of witnesses, let us lay aside every weight, and the sin which doth so easily beset us, and let us run with patience the race that is set before us, ²Looking unto Jesus the author and finisher of our faith; who for the joy that was set before him endured the cross, despising the shame, and is set down at the right hand of the throne of God. ³For consider him that endured such contradiction of sinners against himself, lest ye be wearied and faint in your minds."* We are told to consider Him, which is Jesus Christ! He is the Author and Finisher of our faith. It is Christ who secured our salvation by shedding His precious blood on Calvary's cross. It is Christ who fulfilled the requirements of the Law which we were incapable of doing. He gave us His own righteousness in exchange for our sin! He went to the cross to redeem us from the awful debt of sin we owed. When He died on the cross, He did it for the joy that was set before Him...our salvation, despite our unworthiness. Our passage says that He endured such contradiction of sinners against Himself. This is the same thought behind Romans 5:8, *"But God commendeth his love toward us, in that, while we were yet sinners, Christ died for us."* We were undeserving sinners and yet Christ was willing to die for us that we might be saved. How great a truth that is! It is a truth that should affect how we live! 2 Corinthians 5:14a, *"For the love of*

*Christ constraineth us;*" Because of what He has done and His great love for us, we should feel compelled to live for Him! That is why verse 3 tells us we must not be wearied and faint in our minds. We are to lay aside every weight, which refers to the cares of this life, and the sin which doth so easily beset us, meaning those habitual sins we struggle with on an ongoing basis. We are to live right before God and men. That is what the great cloud of witnesses refers to. Chapter 11, the great hall of faith chapter tells of the believers in the Bible who stood for their faith. Likewise, we are compelled to stand for our Saviour as a testimony to the world. The cloud of witnesses are the same people in the world that witnessed those believers of old. Likewise, the world is witnessing our walk with the Lord today. We need to live right so they see our testimony and receive it. Finally, the race that is set before us is the Christian life which we are to live by looking unto Jesus Christ. Thank God for our blessed Saviour and keep your eyes on Him always!

Woods by a Chateau, Belgium, March 2005

# 26 – Of Whom Shall I Be Afraid?

Psalm 27:1 says, *"The LORD is my light and my salvation; whom shall I fear? the LORD is the strength of my life; of whom shall I be afraid?"* Anxiety and fear are epidemic in our society today! According to statistics from the Anxiety and Depression Association of America, over 40 million American adults are diagnosed with anxiety issues every year. Anxiety disorders afflict 31.9% of American teens from 13 to 18 years old. The world has no hope, and they have every right to fear. Luke 21:26 speaks of the last days saying, *"Men's hearts failing them for fear, and for looking after those things which are coming on the earth: for the powers of heaven shall be shaken."* This world keeps getting darker and more wicked. Fear engulfs its population. They tremble and shake. They turn to drugs and medications to find the relief that only a relationship with Jesus Christ can bring! …But it should not be so with those who walk with the Lord each day. As Christians we have absolutely nothing to fear! Our Bible Gem today tells us that believers in Christ should not be afraid of anything…because the Lord is our strength! In our verse today, David says, *"The LORD is my light and my salvation…"* He is the One who lights our way, so we need not stumble and fall in the darkness of the world. He is our salvation without Whom we would forever be lost! He is our strength from day to day! Romans 8:35 asks us a question along these lines, *"Who shall separate us from the love of Christ? shall tribulation, or distress, or persecution, or famine, or nakedness, or peril, or sword?"* Verses 37-39 answer the question, *"37Nay, in all these things we are more than conquerors through him that loved us. 38For I am persuaded, that neither death, nor life, nor angels, nor principalities, nor powers, nor things present, nor things to come, 39Nor height, nor depth, nor any other creature, shall be able to separate us from the love of God, which is in Christ Jesus our Lord."* When we draw close to our Lord, he removes all fear. Philippians 4:6-7, *"6Be careful for nothing; but in every thing by prayer and supplication with thanksgiving let your requests be made known unto God. 7And the peace of God, which passeth all understanding, shall keep your hearts and minds through Christ Jesus."* Since we are in God's hands, we can give all our cares and fears over to Him and He gives His peace in their place! It is the peace that passeth understanding. The peace the world cannot know! Though the world trembles in fear, the Christian should walk in confidence knowing that they are kept by the Lord.

Ram by the Road, Yukon, Canada, May 2012

# 27 – Asked of God

In 1 Samuel 1:20, the prophet Samuel was born and given his name. That name was given as a testimony of how he came to be born. To understand the significance of this name, we need to go back to the beginning of the chapter. There was a man of Ephraim called Elkanah. His wife, Hannah, was unable to have children and this caused her great distress. Every year Elkanah went up to the city of Shiloh to worship the Lord at the Tabernacle. While in Shiloh, Hannah went to the Tabernacle to pray to the Lord for a son. In verse 11, Hannah made a promise to the Lord. The verse says, *"And she vowed a vow, and said, O LORD of hosts, if thou wilt indeed look on the affliction of thine handmaid, and remember me, and not forget thine handmaid, but wilt give unto thine handmaid a man child, then I will give him unto the LORD all the days of his life, and there shall no razor come upon his head."* She promised that if the Lord would give her a son, she would dedicate him to lifelong service to the Lord. Verse 10 says, *"And she was in bitterness of soul, and prayed unto the LORD, and wept sore."* Her grief and praying were so overwhelming that when Eli, the high priest, saw her, he mistook her actions for drunkenness. In verses 15-16, Hannah explains herself. *"And Hannah answered and said, No, my lord, I am a woman of a sorrowful spirit: I have drunk neither wine nor strong drink, but have poured out my soul before the LORD. Count not thine handmaid for a daughter of Belial: for out of the abundance of my complaint and grief have I spoken hitherto.*" Eli assured her that the Lord had heard her and would answer her prayer. Not long afterward, the Lord did just that! 1 Samuel 1:20 says, "*Wherefore it came to pass, when the time was come about after Hannah had conceived, that she bare a son, and called his name Samuel, saying, Because I have asked him of the LORD.*" The name "*Samuel*" is a Hebrew name that means, "*Asked of God*" or "*Heard of God.*" Hannah named him as a testimony to the fact that God had heard and answered her prayer! When Samuel was still a young child, Hannah brought him to the high priest, Eli, in the Tabernacle where he began his lifelong service to the Lord. He lived his life as a faithful judge, prophet, and priest to the Lord. We, too, serve the same Lord who answers prayer. For those who are trusting Christ as their Savior, we have this recommendation in Hebrews 4:16. "*Let us therefore come boldly unto the throne of grace, that we may obtain mercy, and find grace to help in time of need.*" As believers, we need to know that God wants to hear our prayers and answer them. If we go to Him in faith, we are promised that He will hear us. 1 John 5:14-15, encourages us to pray saying, "*[14]And this is the confidence that we have in him, that, if we ask any thing according to his will, he heareth us: [15]And if we know that he hear us, whatsoever we ask, we know that we have the petitions that we desired of him.*" Trust the Lord who hears your prayers today.

# 28 – Exceeding Great and Precious Promises

2 Peter 1:3-4 reminds us of the promises we have been given by the Lord! The verses speak of God saying, *"³According as his divine power hath given unto us all things that pertain unto life and godliness, through the knowledge of him that hath called us to glory and virtue: ⁴Whereby are given unto us exceeding great and precious promises: that by these ye might be partakers of the divine nature, having escaped the corruption that is in the world through lust."* God has given us many wonderful promises in Scripture! We have the promise of eternal life through faith in Jesus Christ! In Titus 1:2 we find this promise mentioned. *"In hope of eternal life, which God, that cannot lie, promised before the world began;"* God cannot lie, so when He promises something to us, He will make it happen. These promises are secured by God's own infinite power! Verse 3 of our passage starts out, *"According as his divine power hath given unto us all things that pertain unto life and godliness..."* Since God promised and He is almighty, we can trust what He offers us. When we read in Romans 10:13, *"For whosoever shall call upon the name of the Lord shall be saved,"* we know that we have a promise we can count on! We know it because it is God that promised! The promises of God are called *"exceeding great and precious!"* This is because we serve the God that according to Ephesians 3:20 *"...is able to do exceeding*

*abundantly above all that we ask or think...*" We have the promise of His presence in life as we see in Hebrews 13:5, "*...I will never leave thee, nor forsake thee.*" We have the promise of security in His hand. In John 10:28-30 we read, "*28And I give unto them eternal life; and they shall never perish, neither shall any man pluck them out of my hand. 29My Father, which gave them me, is greater than all; and no man is able to pluck them out of my Father's hand. 30I and my Father are one.*" In 1 Peter 1:5, we are told that we "*...are kept by the power of God through faith unto salvation ready to be revealed in the last time.*" There is another side to these promises though. As we begin to understand all that God has promised us in this life and in eternity, it should affect how we live! 2 Corinthians 7:1, "*Having therefore these promises, dearly beloved, let us cleanse ourselves from all filthiness of the flesh and spirit, perfecting holiness in the fear of God.*" God has done so much for us, but what do we do for Him? Living for Him each day is the least we can do in this life. Through these promises we have the power to succeed in living for Him. We often sing the song, "*Standing on the Promises.*" We truly can stand upon the promises of God! Trust in the exceeding great and precious promises of God today!

A Soaring Bald Eagle, Yukon, Canada, May 2012

# 29 – The Power of His Resurrection

Philippians 3:10, *"That I may know him, and the power of his resurrection, and the fellowship of his sufferings, being made conformable unto his death;"* Paul wanted to know Christ more! In the verses leading up to this one Paul has spoken of all the worldly importance and accolades that he had before his salvation and counts them all but dung. He considered them less than useless. To know Christ is all that mattered to him now! This was his entire purpose in life ever since his Damascus road experience, his salvation. How many people do we meet each day and then forget before we see them again? Others we get to know only on a surface level. Paul wanted to know Christ intimately. He wanted to know his heart. He wanted to care about the things that Christ cared about. That is why he wrote what he did! To know Christ was the chief goal of his life!

Not only did he want to know Him, but he wanted to know the power of His resurrection. The resurrection of Christ is the pivotal moment of all world history. No other event in all of time and space has been more important than the resurrection of Jesus Christ. The resurrection is even more important than the crucifixion. Without the resurrection the Lord Jesus was just another martyr for his faith. Without the resurrection, our God is just another dead god. The resurrection changed all that. We do not serve a dead God; we serve a living God! ... And because he lives, we who believe in Him will live also! In Matthew 22:32, the Lord was correcting the Sadducees who denied spiritual things and rejected the idea of a coming resurrection. Quoting what the Father said to Moses, the Lord points out, *"I am the God of Abraham, and the God of Isaac, and the God of Jacob? God is not the God of the dead, but of the living."* He is not the God of the dead, but the God of the living! Because of this, the resurrection of Jesus Christ gives us power for living, for encouragement in serving, and for hope in dying! It is something real that we can cling to in life! It gives us purpose in our lives!

Paul goes on...wanting to know the fellowship of his sufferings. Paul knew that standing for Christ was going to cost him something. The fellowship of Christ's sufferings. Ultimately it cost him his life in Rome, but that cost was not too great for the cause of Christ! Paul was only too happy to pay the price. Let me ask, how much are we willing to pay for our service to Christ? When the trials of our lives come, where do we turn? In Matthew 19:27, the Disciples pointed out that they had left all behind to follow Christ! It is not just the pastor that God calls upon to forsake all and follow Christ, but it is all of us! We need to lay aside the things of this world and seek to know Christ more each day! Knowing Christ in His resurrection and sufferings is the crowning knowledge of all existence!!! It is what each of us should strive for!

# 30 – The Kinsman-Redeemer

You may have heard it said that the Lord Jesus is our Kinsman Redeemer! Do you know what that means? It was a law of Israel given by God in Deuteronomy 25:5-6 and other places in the Old Testament that if a man died and had no children, a close relative was to marry his widow and raise up a child in the name of the deceased so that family line would not be broken. This is the law under which Boaz redeemed Ruth and married her in the beautiful account written of in the book of Ruth. The law also pertained to a Hebrew that was sold into slavery. A close relative could buy back their freedom. In Romans 7:14, Paul speaks of the man without Christ saying, *"For we know that the law is spiritual: but I am carnal, sold under sin."* The Bible teaches that the unsaved person is a slave to sin and if they die in that sin, their eternal destiny is Hell and the Lake of Fire. Our only hope was for our freedom to be purchased. We needed to be redeemed! Based on God's law, this required a Kinsman-Redeemer; a close relative who was willing and able to pay the price for our redemption. That Kinsman-Redeemer is the Lord Jesus Christ!

To fulfill this role, the Lord Jesus had to be our blood relative. That meant He had to be completely human...and He certainly was! Hebrews 4:14-15, *"[14]Seeing then that we have a great high priest, that is passed into the heavens, Jesus the Son of God, let us hold fast our profession. [15]For we have not an high priest which cannot be touched with the feeling of our infirmities; but was in all points tempted like as we are, yet without sin.*" The Lord Jesus took on ordinary human flesh, came to this world, and lived the only perfect life that has ever been lived! He felt hunger. He felt pain. He felt thirst. He felt weariness. His flesh was perfectly human, and yet he lived in it without sin. To reconcile us to God, however, He also had to have God's blood. As the only begotten Son of God, He is God incarnate, that is God in the flesh. As perfect God and perfect man, the Lord was the only One able to pay the price for our redemption.

Thankfully our Lord was not only able, but also willing to pay that price. Romans 5:8 says, "*But God commendeth his love toward us, in that, while we were yet sinners, Christ died for us.*" We were the undeserving sinners sold under the penalty of sin. The Lord Jesus sacrificed His life and shed His precious blood to pay the price of our redemption. It was God's own blood that was shed on Calvary's cross. Christ is the Creator of all things. Therefore, His blood was of more value than all of Creation combined. That is why He can freely offer that payment for sin to whoever comes to Him for salvation! That is how we can trust in the promise of Romans 10:13, "*For whosoever shall call upon the name of the Lord shall be saved.*"

If you have never trusted in Jesus Christ as your personal Saviour, you need to do so today! Acts 16:31 tells us,

"*...Believe on the Lord Jesus Christ, and thou shalt be saved...*" Today if you will repent of your sin...which simply means recognizing yourself as a sinner from the Word of God...and call upon Jesus Christ to save you, believing that He bled and died on the cross for your sins, you will be saved. Please trust in Jesus Christ today and if you do, please give us a call so we can help you find a good church and begin your new life in Christ. You can call us at 502-531-0534.

Tulips by the Moselle River, Metz, France, April 2005

# 31 – Others, Lord, Yes Others!

Who are you living for? Who are you trying to please? Our human nature wants to live for self, but the Bible says we are to do otherwise! In Philippians 2:3-4 we are admonished, "*³Let nothing be done through strife or vainglory; but in lowliness of mind let each esteem other better than themselves. ⁴Look not every man on his own things, but every man also on the things of others.*" Our life is to be lived for others! These verses say we are to "*esteem others better than* [our]*selves.*" This is to say that we are to be more concerned about the needs and desires of others than we are of our own. Our nature is selfish, but the life in Christ is to be one of selflessness! A poem simply called "*Others,*" written by Charles Meigs in the early 1900s and later set to music is a great reminder to us:

> *Lord, help me live from day to day*
> *In such a self-forgetful way*
> *That even when I kneel to pray*
> *My prayer shall be for others.*
>
> ----------------
>
> *Others, Lord, yes others,*
> *Let this my motto be,*
> *Help me to live for others*
> *That I may live like Thee.*

The Lord Jesus did not live for self. He gave His life for us! Galatians 2:20 says, "*I am crucified with Christ: nevertheless I live; yet not I, but Christ liveth in me: and the life which I now live in the flesh I live by the faith of the Son of God, who loved me, and gave himself for me."* Christ loved me and gave His life willingly for me. For that reason, I am crucified with Christ and therefore must die to my selfish desires. The song lyrics pointed out to us that as Christ lived for others, we should also. If this entire world held this Christ-like attitude, it would be a much better place. Ultimately, this mindset is only possible through Christ living in us, and this world is not capable of it. As believers, this should be our motto, *"Others, Lord, yes others."* Achieving selflessness is the great end of Christlikeness. It goes contrary to the desires of the flesh and our nature. Selfishness is the least Christ like attitude we can display! Selfishness will destroy our relationships with both Christ and our fellow man. It destroys marriages, families, and friendships. We will never have a true burden for souls until we learn to focus on others. When we achieve that, we will be what 2 Timothy 2:21 tells us we ought to be. *"If a man therefore purge himself from these, he shall be a vessel unto honour, sanctified, and meet for the master's use, and prepared unto every good work."*

*Others, Lord, yes others,*
*Let this my motto be,*
*Help me to live for others*
*That I may live like Thee.*

# 32 – No Condemnation!

Romans chapter 8 is a wonderful testament to our security as a believer in Christ, Jesus! Verses 1 says, *"There is therefore now no condemnation to them which are in Christ Jesus, who walk not after the flesh, but after the Spirit."* We are reminded here that there is now no condemnation for those who have trusted in Christ! Some suggest that the last part of the verse indicates this promise is conditional on walking in the Spirit. Verse 2 two, however, makes it clear that we are no longer under the death penalty for sin when it says, *"For the law of the Spirit of life in Christ Jesus hath made me free from the law of sin and death."* Walking in the Spirit is the evidence of no longer being under condemnation, not the condition for it. The person without Christ has no ability to walk in the Spirit for the Spirit does not dwell within them. The indwelling of the Spirit of God in the heart of the believer allows us to walk in the Spirit and that testifies to our no longer being under condemnation. What a wonderful truth that we no longer need fear God's wrath! This is not a license to sin, but rather a license to live without fear. Without Christ we live in condemnation. John 3:18 says, *"He that believeth on him is not condemned: but he that believeth not is condemned already, because he hath not believed in the name of the only begotten Son of God."* Praise God our condemnation is taken away in Christ. We have the promise of eternal life...life without end in Heaven! ...And just like it is Christ alone who saved us, it is Christ alone that keeps us saved. There is no separating us from His love. Verses 38-39 of this chapter remind us, *"[38]For I am persuaded, that neither death, nor life, nor angels, nor principalities, nor powers, nor things present, nor things to come, [39]Nor height, nor depth, nor any other creature, shall be able to separate us from the love of God, which is in Christ Jesus our Lord."*

What it means to not be condemned is illustrated in the account of the woman caught in adultery in John chapter 8. This woman was brought before the Lord Jesus in a state of condemnation, under a death sentence. She had no hope and was about to be stoned for her offence. Then the Lord confronted the woman's accusers with their own sin, and they departed one by one leaving the woman alone with Christ. The Lord Jesus then speaks to the woman in John 8:10-11. *"[10]When Jesus had lifted up himself, and saw none but the woman, he said unto her, Woman, where are those thine accusers? hath no man condemned thee? [11]She said, No man, Lord. And Jesus said unto her, Neither do I condemn thee: go, and sin no more."* Her condemnation was taken away through Jesus Christ. This was neither a justification of her sin nor a license to continue in it as the Lord said to *"...go, and sin no more."* Freedom from condemnation allows us to live for God.

What a glorious truth that as believers we are no longer condemned and need not fear the wrath of an angry God. We are now made part of His family, and He deals with us as a loving Father rather than an offended Judge. *"There is* *therefore now <u>no condemnation</u> to them which are in Christ Jesus, who walk not after the flesh, but after the Spirit."*

Acts 14:25, Perga (Perge), Turkey, October 1996

# 33 – Perfect Peace

Many people struggle with fear today. Turmoil in our world strikes fear in the hearts of men. Economic turmoil. Political turmoil. Military turmoil. Luke 21:26 warns of the last days saying, *"Men's hearts failing them for fear, and for looking after those things which are coming on the earth: for the powers of heaven shall be shaken."* This is a good description of people in our world today! This, however, is not where our Bible Gem comes from today. Our Gem is found in Isaiah 26:3 where we are reminded, *"Thou wilt keep him in perfect peace, whose mind is stayed on thee: because he trusteth in thee."* The world may have turmoil and unrest, but in Christ we can have peace…and not only peace, but perfect peace! It is like the lighthouse that stands firm on the rock despite the winds, waves, and storms that beat against it. Those who genuinely trust in the Lord for their strength can have true peace in this life. It is not that we do not experience the same storms, but that we trust in the Lord's protective hand, knowing that He will not allow anything to happen to us that is not in His perfect will. We are not promised immunity from suffering in this life. Not all the prophets were delivered from death, but all had peace in their heart as they went through what God had for them. We can have this same peace through trusting in God. Job suffered tremendously in the book bearing his name, but in the midst of it all we find his statement in Job 13:15. *"Though he slay me, yet will I trust in him: but I will maintain mine own ways before him.*" Though at times Job's faith wavered, his trust in the Lord never broke. Rather his faith was strengthened throughout his trials. David was pursued by King Saul who was bent on killing him, and yet while fleeing and hiding, David wrote some of the most encouraging of the Psalms. Daniel, when faced with the law outlawing his prayers to God did not flinch for a moment but continued praying as before with the windows open. As a result, he spent a night with the lions and an angel from God. Caught between the Red Sea and the army of Pharaoh, Moses trusted the Lord while the people murmured and complained thinking they were about to die. God, of course, did miraculously and the waters were parted. Like Moses, the people should have trusted the Lord, but they did not. The Lord delivered them that they might learn to trust Him. In John 16:33, the Lord Jesus told His disciples, *"These things I have spoken unto you, that in me ye might have peace. In the world ye shall have tribulation: but be of good cheer; I have overcome the world."* This promise was not that they would never experience tribulation, but that they could have peace through it. As we travel this world's shifting seas, we need to learn to trust the Master of the seas, the Lord Jesus. When we truly trust in Him, we can have the perfect peace that God promised to us!

Bird Walking on Ice, Yukon, Canada, May 2012

# 34 – For Our Good

In Romans 8:28, the Apostle Paul encourages us saying, *"And we know that all things work together for good to them that love God, to them who are the called according to his purpose."* But Paul, how could that be when so many bad things happen in the world, even to Christians? Paul would respond, *"Notice that I did not say all things <u>are</u> good, but that they work together <u>for</u> good!"*

It is like baking a birthday cake! It is your birthday, and I invited you to my house. I had you sit at the table where I placed in front of you a stick of butter, a cup of sugar, some raw eggs, two and a half cups of flour, and other ingredients. Then I said enjoy your cake...eat up! You would find the ingredients unpleasant and barely edible. But then if I took all those ingredients, mixed them together in their proper proportions, and baked them for the prescribed time...I could make you a delicious gourmet birthday cake! Likewise, the individual events and circumstances of life can often be unpleasant and painful, but when life is complete, we will find that they all worked together for our good and the good of those around us. These things work according to God's will in ways we often did not recognize beforehand. The life of the patriarch Jacob in the Book of Genesis illustrates this truth wonderfully. Jacob's early life of deceit and trickery caught up with him later in life. He was forced to flee from the murderous wrath of his brother to a foreign land where he himself was deceived. When he finally returned to the land of his fathers, Abraham and Isaac, he went on to have many family problems that never seemed to cease. His beloved Rachel was dead. Joseph seemed to have perished in the clutches of a wild beast. His daughter was defiled by a local prince upon whose city Simeon and Levi had taken murderous revenge. Reuben had committed sin with one of his wives. Simeon was imprisoned in Egypt. Finally, famine was threatening the very lives of his remaining family. Egypt was the only source of food, and its fearsome governor demanded Jacob's youngest son, Benjamin, appear before him before any further supplies would be released. In Genesis 42:36 old Jacob laments, *"Me have ye bereaved of my children: Joseph is not, and Simeon is not, and ye will take Benjamin away: all these things are against me."* He thought all things were against him, but in reality, they were actually working together for the good of his entire family! As the story goes on, it is revealed that the governor was in fact Joseph whom Jacob thought was long dead. Joseph had made provision to save his family from the effects of the famine and to provide them a home in the comforts of Egypt. Later, when reassuring his brothers who were responsible for him being sold into Egypt, Joseph said in Genesis 50:20-21, *"[20]But as for you, ye thought evil against me; but God meant it unto good, to bring to pass, as it is this day, to save much people alive. [21]Now therefore fear ye not: I will nourish you, and your little ones. And he comforted them, and spake kindly unto them."*

When all things seemed to be against Jacob, God was really working things out for his good. It was all according to God's plan, though Jacob failed to see it before the events played out. As we go through life, we encounter many troubles and difficulties even though we may be part of the family of God. It is easy to get discouraged by these circumstances just as Jacob did. When we struggle with the trials of life, we need to remind ourselves of the promise of God in Romans 8:28! *"And we know that all things work together for good to them that love God, to them who are the called according to his purpose."*

Neuschwanstein Castle, Bavaria, Germany, March 2005

# 35 – The Sheep and the Shepherd

*"The LORD is my shepherd; I shall not want."* So begins the 23rd Psalm. It is perhaps the best known and most beloved Psalm of not only Christians, but even the world as a whole. Many unbelievers are familiar with it enough to quote its first verse. As believers, however, we <u>are</u> the sheep the Psalm speaks of. We are the ones who can claim the promises to the sheep in Scripture. In John 10:27-29, the Lord Jesus speaks of His sheep and gives several promises to them. *"$^{27}$My sheep hear my voice, and I know them, and they follow me: $^{28}$And I give unto them eternal life; and they shall never perish, neither shall any man pluck them out of my hand."* As the Lord's sheep, we know the voice of our Saviour though we have never heard it audibly. The Lord's sheep are given eternal life, and we shall never perish. No one can ever pluck us out of our Lord's hand! We never need worry about being pried out of our salvation for it is Christ, the Lord of glory who keeps us!!! In Romans 8:35 Paul begins the verse asking, *"Who shall separate us from the love of Christ?"* He answers his own question in Romans 8:37-39. *"$^{37}$Nay, in all these things we are more than conquerors through him that loved us. $^{38}$For I am persuaded, that neither death, nor life, nor angels, nor principalities, nor powers, nor things present, nor things to come, $^{39}$Nor height, nor depth, nor any other creature, shall be able to separate us from the love of God, which is in Christ Jesus our Lord."* That list pretty much covers everything! <u>Nothing</u> can separate us

from the love of Christ! Nothing can pluck us out of His all-powerful hand! What wonderful promises these are! But Psalm 23 gives us other promises as well. *"The LORD is my shepherd;"* As our Shepherd, the Lord is our guide and protector. *"I shall not want."* He provides our needs that we should not want anything necessary to our lives. *"He maketh me to lie down in green pastures:"* He gives us peace and brings us to the place of His provision. *"he leadeth me beside the still waters."* Sheep hesitate to approach running water and so they need still water to drink. The Lord's provision is always perfect. *"He restoreth my soul:"* We have a renewed spirit through God's Holy Ghost in salvation. *"he leadeth me in the paths of righteousness for his name's sake."* The Lord guides us into His righteousness. *"Yea, though I walk through the valley of the shadow of death, I will fear no evil: for thou art with me; thy rod and thy staff they comfort me."* No harm may befall us without the Lord's approval. His rod and staff both correct us and protect us. *"Thou preparest a table before me in the presence of mine enemies:"* Through Christ we shall prevail against the enemies of the flesh, the world, and the Devil. *"thou anointest my head with oil; my cup runneth over."* The Lord's blessings overflow our ability to contain them all! *"Surely goodness and mercy shall follow me all the days of my life: and I will dwell in the house of the LORD for ever."* Finally, we have blessings throughout our lives and the promise of an eternal abode with our Shepherd. What wonderful comfort we find in the 23rd Psalm!

# 36 – The Blessing of Death

*"16And the LORD God commanded the man, saying, Of every tree of the garden thou mayest freely eat: 17But of the tree of the knowledge of good and evil, thou shalt not eat of it: for in the day that thou eatest thereof thou shalt surely die."* (Genesis 2:16-17). We are all familiar with the account of Adam and Eve and their sin in the Garden of Eden, but you may not realize that death was as much a blessing as a punishment given to mankind because of their failure. In Genesis 3:22-23 we learn the reason man now had to die and why he was forced to leave the Garden of Eden. *"22And the LORD God said, Behold, the man is become as one of us, to know good and evil: and now, lest he put forth his hand, and take also of the tree of life, and eat, and live for ever: 23Therefore the LORD God sent him forth from the garden of Eden, to till the ground from whence he was taken."* The reason God gives for this is that if man did not die, he would live forever as a sinner. He could not be redeemed from the awful consequences of his failure in the Garden! Adam and all his descendants would live forever in sinful, fallen flesh with no hope of redemption. Death allows us to escape this sinful flesh and faith in Christ grants us salvation. 1 John 3:2 tells us, *"Beloved, now are we the sons of God, and it doth not yet appear what we shall be: but we know that, when he shall appear, we shall be like him; for we shall see him as he is."* For those who have trusted in Christ for their eternal salvation, we will one day be with the Lord. This life will

be over, and we will stand before Him. Pain, death, sorrow, and suffering will all be done! If it were not for death, we would simply linger on in a slowly deteriorating world and existence until judgment day. Instead, we have a way to break away from this world of sin. That is why Paul could say in Philippians 1:21, *"For to me to live is Christ, and to die is gain."* If anyone could say that it was Paul. In 2 Corinthians 12, Paul describes a man who was caught up into Heaven and saw its glories. Most who study the Bible believe the man he is speaking of was himself. Paul knew the wonderful life that awaits the believer in Heaven. Death can be a sad occasion. It is a time of parting, and we often feel lonely and saddened when our loved ones pass, but to the child of God, death is nothing to be afraid of. It is the time we finally rest from the toils of this life and receive the eternal comfort provided by our Saviour. Revelation 21:3-4 says, *"³And I heard a great voice out of heaven saying, Behold, the tabernacle of God is with men, and he will dwell with them, and they shall be his people, and God himself shall be with them, and be their God. ⁴And God shall wipe away all tears from their eyes; and there shall be no more death, neither sorrow, nor crying, neither shall there be any more pain: for the former things are passed away."* The beloved song *"My Savior First of All,"* by Fanny Crosby (1894), reminds us of the joys to be found for the Christian beyond the grave.

*When my lifework is ended and I cross the swelling tide,*
*When the bright and glorious morning I shall see;*

*I shall know my Redeemer when I reach the other side,
And His smile will be the first to welcome me.*

Death for those in Christ is simply the doorway into the presence of our dear Lord and the wonderful existence He has prepared for us.

"Big Ben" Clock Tower, London, England, March 2002

# 37 – Words of Comfort

This life and this world can be depressing at times, and we all need to receive comfort. Paul recognized this when he reminded us in 2 Corinthians 1:3-4, *"³Blessed be God, even the Father of our Lord Jesus Christ, the Father of mercies, and the God of all comfort; ⁴Who comforteth us in all our tribulation, that we may be able to comfort them which are in any trouble, by the comfort wherewith we ourselves are comforted of God."* Paul calls our Father in Heaven the *"God of all comfort; Who comforteth us in all our tribulation."* God loves us and comforts us. He truly understands us as well. Hebrews 4:15 speaks of the Lord Jesus saying, *"For we have not an high priest which cannot be touched with the feeling of our infirmities; but was in all points tempted like as we are, yet without sin."* He experienced life as we do. It says that He suffered the same infirmities that we deal with each day. He felt hunger. He felt pain. He felt weariness and heartache. All the things we deal with here on Earth, He experienced them all! He knows how we feel. Because of this, He knows just how to comfort us as well. 2 Thessalonians 2:16-17, *"Now our Lord Jesus Christ himself, and God, even our Father, which hath loved us, and hath given us everlasting consolation and good hope through grace, Comfort your hearts, and stablish you in every good word and work."* This world can offer us no comfort and usually gives us misery for our trouble. Christ, however, gives comfort and consolation. He does this personally through His Word and as well as through other people. Our verses in 2 Corinthians say that one of the reasons He comforts us is so that we can, in turn, give that same comfort to others. In verse 4 Paul says of God, *"Who comforteth us in all our tribulation, that we may be able to comfort them which are in any trouble, by the comfort wherewith we ourselves are comforted of God."* When we are comforted by God, it is His intention that we share that comfort with someone else. God's comfort is not for us to consume, but for us to share! Philippians 2:4 advises us, *"Look not every man on his own things, but every man also on the things of others."* God comforts us because He loves us, and He commands us to love one another also. John 13:35, *"By this shall all men know that ye are my disciples, if ye have love one to another."* We demonstrate our love in how we treat each other, and that is particularly important when someone is suffering. We need to comfort those that weep. Romans 12:15, *"Rejoice with them that do rejoice, and weep with them that weep."* The testimony and encouragement of someone who has been through what you are going through can certainly help in hard times. Ultimately, though, it is God that gives true comfort. His Holy Spirit is called the Comforter. To a world lost in sin, the salvation provided through Christ's shed blood and revealed to us through His Spirit is the ultimate comfort we can receive. We also have many precious promises in the Scriptures that we can claim and receive comfort from. Our God is truly the God of all comfort. He loves us and cares for us and comforts us in our time of need! As a child of God through Christ, you can turn to Him at any time, and He promises to be there with us. In the last part of Hebrews 13:5, we are told, *"for he hath said, I will never leave thee, nor forsake thee."* Our God is always there for us, and we must take comfort in that solace.

The Eastern Gate, Jerusalem, Israel, June 2007

# 38 – New Life in Christ

As believers in Christ, we need to lead pure lives before the Lord. The unbelieving world does as it pleases and plumbs the very depths of sin. Christians must not live that way! Believing on Christ is not simply *"turning over a new leaf"* but it is a change of heart and a new life. 2 Corinthians 5:17 says, *"Therefore if any man be in Christ, he is a new creature: old things are passed away; behold, all things are become new."* When a person gets saved, they are changed and brought to spiritual life where they were spiritually dead before. Things that they valued before become meaningless and what they cared nothing for has now become their passion. This does not mean we stop sinning altogether, but our attitude towards sin will change. I had a friend when I was in the military stationed in Japan. He got saved and then a couple of weeks later he was working a long shift under difficult conditions and lost his temper. He yelled at some of the mechanics working for him and used some bad language. Later in the evening he came to me and told me that he must not really be saved because Christians don't speak and act that way. I kind of chuckled as I told him he was right that he should not lose his temper or use foul language. Then I told him that does not mean he is not saved, and I asked him a question to prove it. I said, *"If you had done that two weeks ago, would you have cared?"* *"Not in the least,"* he replied. The difference was not that he did not occasionally fall back into his old ways, but rather that he was no longer comfortable in that behavior. That discomfort is one of the ways God prompts us to change that behavior and submit to the new nature He has placed in us at salvation. Romans 6:4 tells us, *"Therefore we are buried with him by baptism into death: that like as Christ was raised up from the dead by the glory of the Father, even so we also should walk in newness of life."* God wants us to have a changed life after we get saved, but it is not achieved through our own efforts, but by yielding to His Holy Spirit in our lives. Paul goes on in Romans 6:12-13, *"[12]Let not sin therefore reign in your mortal body, that ye should obey it in the lusts thereof. [13]Neither yield ye your members as instruments of unrighteousness unto sin: but yield yourselves unto God, as those that are alive from the dead, and your members as instruments of righteousness unto God."* We are to give God control of our lives so that we can achieve the life He desires for us. This yielding, however, goes against our flesh which is by nature selfish and wants control. For the Christian, there is always a struggle going on within us. A struggle between the old nature and the new. Each day we need to renew our commitment to being yielded unto God. One thing that can make this struggle more difficult is a failure to remove bad influences from our lives. In Romans 13:14, we are directed, *"But put ye on the Lord Jesus Christ, and make not provision for the flesh, to fulfil the lusts thereof."* We make *"provision"* for the flesh by going back to the same places we used to, or by keeping things around us that will tempt us. When we begin to grow in Christ, we will begin to have convictions about removing old things from our lives. For instance, if I decide the music I used to listen to was not honoring to God, and I take it all and put it in a box in the attic instead of destroying it and throwing it away, I have made provision for the flesh. In a weak moment, the music will still be in the box ready to be pulled out to draw me back into my old life that should be gone for good. As believers, we need to live pure lives that are pleasing to God. Because of the change He makes in us at salvation we have the power to live that life as we yield unto Him. If you are not saved today, you have no defense against the lusts and whims of the flesh. You need to trust Christ as your Savior! Acts 16:31 tells us, *"believe on the Lord Jesus Christ, and thou shalt be saved!"* You need to see yourself as a lost, Hell bound sinner and recognize that Christ died to pay for your sin. Call on Him in prayer. Ask Him to save you and He promises He will. Romans 10:13 says, *"For whosoever shall call upon the name of the Lord shall be saved."*

Temple Mount and Dome of the Rock, Jerusalem, Israel, June 2007

# 39 – God Is in Control

We are naturally shortsighted people! We cannot see and often not even perceive spiritual realities. As a result, we are sometimes driven to despair over circumstances we cannot control! We must keep in mind that when this world seems out of control, God is still at the helm and watching over us. It is all still under His command. We need not fear. That was the situation in our Bible Gem today. In 2 Kings chapter 6, the army of Syria was attacking the northern kingdom of Israel. The king of Syria was commanding the army, and they decided that they needed to eliminate the prophet of God before they could destroy the Israeli army. The Syrian army was powerful and there seemed to be little hope for the prophet Elisha and those few with him. Elisha's servant feared for their survival and cried out to the prophet. 2 Kings 6:15-17 says, *"15And when the servant of the man of God was risen early, and gone forth, behold, an host compassed the city both with horses and chariots. And his servant said unto him, Alas, my master! how shall we do? 16And he answered, Fear not: for they that be with us are more than they that be with them. 17And Elisha prayed, and said, LORD, I pray thee, open his eyes, that he may see. And the LORD opened the eyes of the young man; and he saw: and, behold, the mountain was full of horses and chariots of fire round about Elisha."* The servant only saw the army of Syria, but the spiritual reality was that the army of God had encamped about the whole area! They were providing an unseen defense that the servants of God could rely upon! Elisha then asked God to smite the Syrian army with blindness. The prophet then led the army and their king captive into Samaria, the capital of the northern kingdom of Israel. Elisha understood that when all seemed lost, God still had everything under His control. The same can be said in our lives! When it seems that our world is crashing down around us, we need not fear because God is still watching over us. A verse I frequently quote, Romans 8:28, tells us, *"And we know that all things work together for good to them that love God, to them who are the called according to his purpose."* Individual circumstances may not be good for us, but we have God's promise that they will all work together for our good, either here and now, or in eternity. What Christ has promised us is that He would go through it all with us. In the last part of Hebrews 13:5 we are reminded, *"...for he hath said, I will never leave thee, nor forsake thee."* No, that does not mean that everything is going to come up roses. Rather it means that everything will work out according to God's will and purposes, as well as to our eternal benefit. Remember, God did not deliver all the prophets from death. For that reason, Paul reminds us in Philippians 1:21, *"For to me to live is Christ, and to die is gain."* In the book of Exodus Israel was backed up against the Red Sea with the mountains all around and Pharaoh's army in hot pursuit. Israel cried in frustration against Moses for leading them to their demise! The situation seemed hopeless, but Moses understood the truth of our Bible Gem today. God was still in control. Moses' reply to the people is found in Exodus 14:13-14, *"¹³And Moses said unto the people, Fear ye not, stand still, and see the salvation of the LORD, which he will shew to you to day: for the Egyptians whom ye have seen to day, ye shall see them again no more for ever. ¹⁴The LORD shall fight for you, and ye shall hold your peace."* God then parted the Red Sea so that Israel could pass through on dry land. Pharaoh's army attempted to follow them only to find that they did not have Israel's God on their side. The sea was allowed to fall back down upon them, and they all drowned, but Israel was saved by the hand of God. Whatever you are going through today, know that if you are saved through knowing Christ as your Savior, you need fear nothing. If you have never trusted in Jesus Christ, you are in the situation of Pharaoh's army and in danger of God's judgment. You need to believe on Jesus Christ as your personal Savior today and then you too will enjoy His care and provision both now and in eternity. If you have any questions or want to learn more about salvation, please call Lighthouse Baptist Church at 502-531-0534. We would be glad to tell you how to be saved and get you started down the road on your new Christian life. If you are saved today then just trust that God has everything under control, and that He's going to take care of you and provide for you every day of your life. Then He will provide you with a home in Heaven for all eternity.

# 40 – Ten Lepers

As I write this Bible Gem, we are celebrating Thanksgiving in America. It is the time we set aside other concerns to be thankful for the things God has done in our lives. It is a worthy thought, but the question is, are we truly thankful? Thankfulness goes against human nature which in essence is quite selfish. In Luke 17 we see this perfectly illustrated in the account of the 10 lepers. The Lord Jesus was passing between Samaria and Galilee on His way to Jerusalem. As He entered a village along the way, He was met by 10 lepers that begged to be healed. Leprosy was a terrible disease that was common in the first century. When a person was diagnosed with the highly contagious disease, their life as they knew it was at an end. They were cast out of society into a place apart where they would remain until they very slowly died. In Luke 17:14, the Lord reacts to their request. *"And when he saw them, he said unto them, Go shew yourselves unto the priests. And it came to pass, that, as they went, they were cleansed."* Praise God! The Lord had mercy on these ten and cleansed them of their terrible leprosy. What happened next, however, is very telling in regards to the human condition. Luke 17:15-16, *"[15]And one of them, when he saw that he was healed, turned back, and with a loud voice glorified God, [16]And fell down on his face at his feet, giving him thanks: and he was a Samaritan."* One of them was so overcome by what was done for him, that he rushed back to give thanks. The Lord Jesus observed in Luke

17:17-18, *"¹⁷And Jesus answering said, Were there not ten cleansed? but where are the nine? ¹⁸There are not found that returned to give glory to God, save this stranger."* Of the ten who were cleansed, only one displayed thankfulness. 1 Timothy 3:1-2 tells us several attributes of people in the last days. One of those attributes is that they will be unthankful. We need to be thankful people, especially in regard to what God has done for us. In Scripture, the disease of leprosy is figuratively used to represent man's sinful nature. When the Lord Jesus physically cleansed these lepers, it was also a spiritual picture of salvation and the cleansing from the filth of sin from our lives. The ten lepers all experienced the outward cleansing of the flesh, but the one that came back to praise God also received spiritual cleansing. In verse 19 of our passage we read, *"And he said unto him, Arise, go thy way: thy faith hath made thee whole."* This individual was cleansed inwardly as well. Ephesians 2:8-9 tells us, *"⁸For by grace are ye saved through faith; and that not of yourselves: it is the gift of God: ⁹Not of works, lest any man should boast."* We are saved through faith alone by God's grace. This leper had demonstrated that saving faith and was made whole. When we believe on Jesus Christ, that He died on the cross to pay for our sins and then rose on the third day, we have God's promise of salvation. Like the leper, we are cleansed spiritually and given new life in Christ. Also like the leper, we need to show our thanks and gratefulness to the Lord both verbally and through living our lives for Him.

# 41 – The Faith of Noah

Hebrews chapter 11 has often been called the *"Hall of Faith"* because it mentions all the heroes of our faith we read about in Scripture. When we talk about individuals in the Bible who had great faith, we usually think of Abraham, David, Job, and others. Noah is not often one of the first names that come to mind, and yet he is mentioned prominently in God's list in this chapter! Hebrews 11:7 says, *"By faith Noah, being warned of God of things not seen as yet, moved with fear, prepared an ark to the saving of his house; by the which he condemned the world, and became heir of the righteousness which is by faith."* There is much in this one verse that reveals the importance of Noah's faith! The time of Noah was a time of great wickedness! Genesis 6:5-6 says, *"⁵And God saw that the wickedness of man was great in the earth, and that every imagination of the thoughts of his heart was only evil continually. ⁶And it repented the LORD that he had made man on the earth, and it grieved him at his heart."* God determined that it was time to judge the earth for its wickedness. Only Noah was able to find grace and salvation in the sight of God. God's grace has always only been appropriated by faith, and that faith is what places Noah in the list of Hebrews 11. Noah's entry in the chapter begins by pointing out that he was *"warned of God of things not seen as yet."* The world had never seen anything like the Flood before. To believe that a judgment of this magnitude was even possible took great faith. Many have suggested that the Bible even teaches that there was no rain whatsoever before the Flood! Genesis 2:5 tells us, *"And every plant of the field before it was in the earth, and every herb of the field before it grew: for the LORD God had not caused it to rain upon the earth, and there was not a man to till the ground."* In fact, it was only after the Flood that God placed the rainbow in the sky. Noah believed what to the world seemed unbelievable. Noah built the Ark on dry ground before the first drop of rain ever wet its surface.

It was through faith that Noah was saved. He was physically saved because he did not perish with the rest of the world in the Flood. He was also spiritually saved by his faith. Our verse tells us, he *"became heir of the righteousness which is by faith."* 2 Corinthians 5:21, speaking of our relationship to Christ, tells us, *"For he hath made him to be sin for us, who knew no sin; that we might be made the righteousness of God in him."* Our righteousness in God comes from faith in Jesus Christ, not from our good works.

Noah's faith also affected those around him. His family also believed and joined him in the Ark. We are told that he *"prepared an ark to the saving of his house."* His family followed his faith and thus were saved as well. There was, however, another effect. The verse says next, *"by the which he condemned the world."* For God to destroy the Earth leaving no one behind would derail His plan to provide the Saviour whom we know as Jesus Christ. All of mankind would have been beyond redemption. That meant that God had to preserve some human life through the Flood. He did so through Noah and his family. But it was Noah's obedience by faith that made this possible. Had Noah not built the Ark, God could not proceed with the Flood. Now, I am not suggesting that God's plan could so easily be disrupted, because he knew Noah would obey before He told him anything. Rather I am pointing out that Noah's obedience was a necessary part of God's plan. That is how the verse can say of his faith, *"by the which he condemned the world."* The world could be condemned because Noah believed and obeyed.

As believers in Christ, we too need to live by the same faith Noah had. We are to believe God even when it seems unbelievable. We need to recognize that our faith will also affect our family. We must finally understand the sobering truth that our living by faith will be part of the condemnation of this world in the judgment. Noah is one of the great heroes of our faith and we need to follow in his footsteps and believe God!

The Valley of Jezreel (Armageddon), Jerusalem, Israel, June 2007

# 42 – Forgetting Those Things

We like to reminisce. We reminisce about past success, and sometimes also dwell on our past failures. In Philippians 3:13-14, Paul warns us about doing this. He says, *"[13]Brethren, I count not myself to have apprehended: but this one thing I do, forgetting those things which are behind, and reaching forth unto those things which are before, [14]I press toward the mark for the prize of the high calling of God in Christ Jesus."* Paul advises us to do three things. First, we must put the past behind us, *"...forgetting those things which are behind..."* As Christians, we are all nothing more than sinners saved by grace! We have a past that can haunt us from time to time. We look back on all our mistakes in life and wish we could change them...but we can't! We must learn from these failures and do our best to put them behind us. Likewise, when we succeed, we can rejoice in it for a moment but then we must move on. Dwelling too long on our accomplishments can be as debilitating to us as dwelling on failure because it causes us to coast along on past victories. This begs the age-old question, *"What have you done for me lately?"* The problem with being stuck in the past is that we often become useless in the present. If anyone could live on past success (and likewise failures), it was the Apostle Paul. He gives us a clear admonition to never do that. The past is there for us to learn from and nothing more. Learn from the past, good or bad, and then move on.

Secondly, Paul tells us to look to the future: *"...reaching forth unto those things which are before..."* We have the promise of a home in Heaven with the Lord! The Lord Jesus is coming again to take us there. Titus 2:13, *"Looking for that blessed hope, and the glorious appearing of the great God and our Saviour Jesus Christ;"* When He comes, He will also reward us for our faithfulness. Hebrews 6:10, *"For God is not unrighteous to forget your work and labour of love, which ye have shewed toward his name, in that ye have ministered to the saints, and do minister."* There is a brighter day coming! Even looking forward, though, there is something we need to consider even more.

Paul finishes his thought by pointing out that, most importantly, we are to act in the present. Verse 14 says, *"I press toward the mark for the prize of the high calling of God in Christ Jesus."* There is much work left to do in this world! God does not take us home the moment we get saved because He has work for each of us to do! You say, "Brother Bill, what can I do for the Lord? I can't do much." That is not true! There is much each of us can do, no matter what our situation! You can pray. You can witness to someone. You can read God's Word. You can live for Him. You can love your neighbor. You can memorize Scripture. The most important day in serving Christ is today! We may have plans for tomorrow, but there are opportunities today!!! The Lord warned in John 9:4, *"I must work the works of him that sent me, while it is day:*

*the night cometh, when no man can work."* Time is short. We must work for the Lord now. In John 4:35 the Lord reminds us, *"Say not ye, There are yet four months, and then cometh harvest? behold, I say unto you, Lift up your eyes, and look on the fields; for they are white already to harvest."* There are souls to be rescued from eternal damnation. Paul calls what we are striving for in this life, *"...the prize of the high calling of God in Christ Jesus."* There is nothing more important in this life than serving Christ! It is the greatest work possible in our existence. We expend so much effort for the world, but how much for the Lord? What we do for the Lord is of eternal value. We need to get over our past, set our sights on the future, and work in the present if we are going to accomplish anything for God! We must *"...press toward the mark for the prize of the high calling of God in Christ Jesus."*

Palm Tree on the Beach, Punta Salinas, Dominican Republic, December 2024

# 43 – Closeness with God

Many believers struggle with feeling close to God. They ask me how to overcome that. I believe there are three main reasons why people feel this way. The first hinderance to feeling close to God is sin! In James 4:8 we are encouraged to, *"Draw nigh to God, and he will draw nigh to you. Cleanse your hands, ye sinners; and purify your hearts, ye double minded."* God is never further from us than we are from Him. The closer we try to get to God, the closer He is to us. This verse, however, is conditional on us cleansing ourselves from sin. David warns us in Psalm 66:18, *"If I regard iniquity in my heart, the Lord will not hear me:"* We need to make sure a sin problem isn't what keeps us from feeling close to God.

The second cause can be looking to man rather than God for our faith. People will let you down, but God never will. Hebrews 12:2 reminds us we are to be, *"Looking unto Jesus the author and finisher of our faith."*

Though these two problems will cause a feeling of distance from God in the Christian life, the third is the one I believe is usually the person's problem. They aren't spending enough time alone with God. Are you feeling like God is far away from you? How much time are you spending with the Lord in His Word and in prayer? More than anything, I think this is our problem. We don't have enough *"quiet time"* with God. We get busy about the business of this world and don't spend enough time with our Father in Heaven. If you did not spend much time with your spouse, you would not feel close to them either. So why do we find it odd when we do not feel close to God when we spend very little time with Him?

In Psalm 1 we are told about the life of the blessed man. It tells us, *"But his delight is in the law of the LORD; and in his law doth he meditate day and night."* The whole of Psalm 119, which, incidentally, is the longest chapter in the entire Bible, talks extensively about the benefits of reading, studying, and memorizing God's Word. The more time we spend in God's Word and thinking on it throughout the day, the more we will begin to understand and appreciate the Lord. Add to that 1 Thessalonians 5:17 which says, *"Pray without ceasing,"* and you will have a recipe for closeness with the Lord. When we say, *"Pray without ceasing,"* we are not talking about formal prayer, but rather just talking to God as you go through the day. As things happen in life, just have in your thoughts that God is with you and speak to Him in your heart during the events of the day. The more time you spend in His Word and with this attitude of prayer, the more you will be aware of His presence and the closer you will walk with Him.

Before David became king of Israel, he had to flee for his life from jealous King Saul. Saul knew that God had rejected him as king and that David would succeed him rather than his son Jonathan. For this reason, Saul was driven to a murderous rage against David. As David fled from Saul, he often struggled with his trust in God. In

Psalm 13:1-2 David cries out, *"¹How long wilt thou forget me, O LORD? for ever? how long wilt thou hide thy face from me? ²How long shall I take counsel in my soul, having sorrow in my heart daily? how long shall mine enemy be exalted over me?"* Because of the trials he was going through, David felt distant from God. In verses 3 and 4 he prays, *"³Consider and hear me, O LORD my God: lighten mine eyes, lest I sleep the sleep of death; ⁴Lest mine enemy say, I have prevailed against him; and those that trouble me rejoice when I am moved."* But finally in verses 5-6 David remembers his closeness to God! *"⁵But I have trusted in thy mercy; my heart shall rejoice in thy salvation. ⁶I will sing unto the LORD, because he hath dealt bountifully with me."* If you want to have a close relationship with the Lord, the key is to spend adequate time in His Word and pray at all times throughout the day.

Snorkeling in the Caribbean Sea, Antigua, December 2005

# 44 – Revive Us Again!

The author of Psalm 85 cries out to God in verse 6, *"Wilt thou not revive us again: that thy people may rejoice in thee?"* The psalmist recognized that the nation of Israel had become cold toward God and needed to be revived. He was crying out to God to restore to the nation the spiritual life that they once had. Our churches today are suffering from the same spiritual coldness. A preacher once asked the question, *"If the Holy Spirit left our churches, would our programs still go on?"* Sadly, we would probably never even notice. We have learned to do the ministry without the power of God. We follow formulas rather than the Spirit. Like Samson of old, we are going out, not even realizing that God is not with us! Judges 16:20, *"And she said, The Philistines be upon thee, Samson. And he awoke out of his sleep, and said, I will go out as at other times before, and shake myself. And he wist not that the LORD was departed from him."* We are at risk of doing the very same thing today and we need spiritual revival!

2 Chronicles 7:14 has often been called God's *"formula for revival."* As always, we go looking for formulas rather than seeking the Lord. In this case, the formula is to seek the Lord, so it is good advice! The verse reads, *"If my people, which are called by my name, shall humble themselves, and pray, and seek my face, and turn from their wicked ways; then will I hear from heaven, and will*

*forgive their sin, and will heal their land.*" This promise was given to King Solomon and Israel in the Old Testament, but the principle still applies today. The Lord says, "*If my people, which are called by my name...*" Today, the people called by the Lord's name refers to the true Bible-believing, born again Christians. We as believers in Christ must meet God's requirements to see revival in our churches. The Lord then explains what these requirements are. "*...shall humble themselves...*" Who are we as sinners to stand before the most holy God? We must come to Him in humility recognizing that Christ's work on the cross is the only reason we have any right to come to Him at all. "*...and pray...*" We can demand nothing of the Lord, but He delights in our humble prayers. "*...and seek my face...*" It is only to the Lord we can come for this refreshing! "*...and turn from their wicked ways...*" This is the part we have trouble with. We love to hold on to our wicked ways. We conform our lives to the world rather than the Word of God. We watch television shows that glorify the very things Christ died for. We act no different than the world when we go off to work and play each day. We fail to testify for Christ in this lost and dying world. 1 Peter 1:16 admonishes us, "*Because it is written, Be ye holy; for I am holy.*" How holy is God? Absolutely holy! We will never be that holy in this life, but we rarely even make the effort to try. How much holiness are we satisfied with in our lives?

The Lord then tells us the result of this kind of holy prayer! *"...then will I hear from heaven, and will forgive their sin, and will heal their land."* God will send revival upon us! I have heard this preached many times, but I have rarely heard the opposite truth preached. If it is true that praying in this fashion results in revival in the land, then it must also be true that a lack of such revival means that God's people have failed to do what he asks of them. We cannot truly blame the world for the state of our nations. It is not the fault of the schools, or the government, or the entertainment industry. These are merely symptoms of the actual problem. If our world is in a state of moral decline, the fault lies with the church! If we fail to *"...humble* [our]*selves, and pray, and seek* [His] *face, and turn from* [our] *wicked ways;"* then we will never see revival come to our land! Our nations will continue their fall into wickedness until we as God's people clean up our lives and get on our faces before Him! The question today is, "are we willing to pay the price for revival in our land?"

The Harding Icefield near Seward, Alaska, August 2012

# 45 – The Weapons of Our Warfare

We are at war! It is a war as real as if there was gunfire all around us. We don't notice because it is a spiritual war, but we are fighting in it every day! As good soldiers of Jesus Christ, we need to know our weapons and be trained in their use! 2 Corinthians 10:4 describes our weapons. It says, *"(For the weapons of our warfare are not carnal, but mighty through God to the pulling down of strong holds;)"* We are not fighting with carnal weapons such as guns and swords, but with the mighty weapons of God! Our weapons are God's Word, and prayer, and faith!!! They are perfect weapons for the spiritual combat we face each day!

The primary offensive weapon of the soldier of the Lord is God's Word. Hebrews 4:12 says, *"For the word of God is quick, and powerful, and sharper than any twoedged sword, piercing even to the dividing asunder of soul and spirit, and of the joints and marrow, and is a discerner of the thoughts and intents of the heart."* It is the most effective spiritual weapon on the battlefield. It is quick, meaning it is alive! It is not some musty old book that has no meaning for today. It has cut to the heart of people in every age of mankind throughout history. It reveals our sinfulness and our need for a Saviour, Jesus Christ. It is powerful, even overcoming Satan and his minions. It was the Word of God that our Lord used to defeat Satan during His temptation in the wilderness. It is razor sharp and cuts deep enough to convict us unto salvation!

Prayer is another of our spiritual weapons! It is also a very powerful weapon. Jeremiah 33:3 encourages us to call upon God in prayer. Jeremiah tells us, *"Call unto me, and I will answer thee, and show thee great and mighty things, which thou knowest not."* It is also a positive weapon. We think of weapons as being solely destructive, but not so with God's weapons! James 5:15 promises us, *"And the prayer of faith shall save the sick, and the Lord shall raise him up; and if he have committed sins, they shall be forgiven him."* It is also an unlimited weapon because it depends upon the power of God and not man! In Matthew 21:22, the Lord Jesus promises us, *"And all things, whatsoever ye shall ask in prayer, believing, ye shall receive."*

Finally, we have our primary defensive weapon, faith! Faith is the weapon that protects us. In Ephesians 6:16, Paul reminds us, *"Above all, taking the shield of faith, wherewith ye shall be able to quench all the fiery darts of the wicked."* The devil is always on the attack hurling his fiery darts in our direction. The only way to stop those attacks is with the shield of faith! Left to ourselves we would be easy prey for the devil. In 1 Peter 5:8 we are warned, *"Be sober, be vigilant; because your adversary the devil, as a roaring lion, walketh about, seeking whom he may devour:"* The devil is like a powerful lion, but the shield of faith is more powerful. It is strong enough to resist his onslaught. This is because faith is based on God's ability and not our own. Through faith we can conquer!

Hebrews 11:33 tells of the faith of the saints of old saying, *"Who through faith subdued kingdoms, wrought righteousness, obtained promises, stopped the mouths of lions,"* It is the Lord that gives us the victory.

Romans 8:31 says, *"What shall we then say to these things? If God be for us, who can be against us?"* Verses 35-39 of that passage go on to encourage us saying, *"[35]Who shall separate us from the love of Christ? shall tribulation, or distress, or persecution, or famine, or nakedness, or peril, or sword? [36]As it is written, For thy sake we are killed all the day long; we are accounted as sheep for the slaughter. [37]Nay, in all these things we are more than conquerors through him that loved us. [38]For I am persuaded, that neither death, nor life, nor angels, nor principalities, nor powers, nor things present, nor things to come, [39]Nor height, nor depth, nor any other creature, shall be able to separate us from the love of God, which is in Christ Jesus our Lord."*

We are in a spiritual war every day fighting the forces of evil that seek to destroy us and the world we live in, but God has equipped us to fight and win the war. We just need to put on the whole armor of God and pick up the weapons He gives us to use. Then we need to go out and fight the battle because He has already promised us the victory!

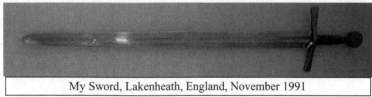

My Sword, Lakenheath, England, November 1991

# 46 – Borrow not a Few!

In 2 Kings chapter 4 we read of the wife of one of the prophets, which is what preachers were called in the time of Elisha. The prophet had died leaving a large debt. Now the creditor was coming to take her sons to be bondmen in order to work off the debt. The widow went to Elisha to ask for help. Verses 2-4 say, "*²And Elisha said unto her, What shall I do for thee? tell me, what hast thou in the house? And she said, Thine handmaid hath not any thing in the house, save a pot of oil. ³Then he said, Go, borrow thee vessels abroad of all thy neighbours, even empty vessels; borrow not a few. ⁴And when thou art come in, thou shalt shut the door upon thee and upon thy sons, and shalt pour out into all those vessels, and thou shalt set aside that which is full.*" Elisha gave the woman some instructions on what to do as the Lord was about to perform a miracle on their behalf…but notice what Elisha told her at the end of verse 3, "*borrow not a few.*" We'll come back to that. In verses 5-6 we read, "*⁵So she went from him, and shut the door upon her and upon her sons, who brought the vessels to her; and she poured out. ⁶And it came to pass, when the vessels were full, that she said unto her son, Bring me yet a vessel. And he said unto her, There is not a vessel more. And the oil stayed.*" She and her sons obeyed the man of God and saw God work miraculously! In verse 7 she returns to Elisha, "*Then she came and told the man of God. And he said, Go, sell the oil, and pay thy debt, and live thou and thy children of the rest.*" God had provided for the need of this desperate widow, but there are a few things we can learn from this passage.

First, remember the prophet told her to "*borrow not a few.*" Elisha was telling her that God was going to miraculously provide for her need, but she needed to demonstrate her measure of faith through her works. By faith, she was to borrow these vessels. If she borrowed only a few, there would only be a little oil provided. Notice that the miracle stopped when the last vessel was filled. Thankfully she listened to Elisha and borrowed many! Because of her faith, as seen through the number of vessels she borrowed, she received more than enough to pay the debt. She then had enough excess on which to continue to live long after the miracle! Sometimes the limit on what God will do in our lives is how much faith we demonstrate. God is often willing to do much more with us, but it is our unbelief that limits the outcome. It is certainly not God's ability or even His desire that limits us in the Christian life!

In contrast to this event in the ministry of Elisha, we have another that occurred near the end of his life. In 2 Kings chapter 13, the King of Israel had come to Elisha to pay his respects before the man of God passed from this life. Elisha, wanting God to do something for the king, told the king to take a bow and shoot arrows at the ground that would represent Israel's deliverance from her enemies. The king shot three arrows and stopped. Verse 19 tells us the prophet's reaction, "*And the man of God was wroth with him, and said, Thou shouldest have smitten five or six times; then hadst thou smitten Syria till thou hadst consumed it: whereas now thou shalt smite Syria but thrice.*" Unlike the widow who demonstrated her faith by borrowing many vessels, the king shot only a few times and thus was deprived by his lack of faith from seeing what God might have otherwise done.

In the Christian life, God wants to work miraculously in us and through us. It is only our faith that limits what God will do. Trust Him more fully today and seek Him in prayer. In response, God gives us the assurance in Jeremiah 33:3, *"Call unto me, and I will answer thee, and shew thee great and mighty things, which thou knowest not."*

Snowy Forest, Yukon, Canada, May 2012

# 47 – The Battle Is the Lord's

King Jehoshaphat of Judah was a godly king. In 2 Chronicles 20, he and the southern kingdom of Judah were under attack from the nations of Moab, Ammon, and Mount Seir. The Bible says that Jehoshaphat was afraid, which caused him and the people to seek the Lord in prayer. The Lord responded through a prophet in verses 15 and 17. *"¹⁵And he said, Hearken ye, all Judah, and ye inhabitants of Jerusalem, and thou king Jehoshaphat, Thus saith the LORD unto you, Be not afraid nor dismayed by reason of this great multitude; for the battle is not yours, but God's…¹⁷Ye shall not need to fight in this battle: set yourselves, stand ye still, and see the salvation of the LORD with you, O Judah and Jerusalem: fear not, nor be dismayed; to morrow go out against them: for the LORD will be with you."* Israel had sought the Lord and He had heard them. God reminded His people who is on the throne in Heaven and who it is that fought for them! The Lord said He would be the One defending them! The king heard and believed the Lord's promise! Such was the faith and trust of Jehoshaphat in the Lord, that the next day, instead of arraying his army for battle, he sent singers and musicians in front of his troops as they approached the enemy. When they arrived at the battlefield, they found that the three armies had wiped each other out. God had turned their hearts against one another so completely that not one soldier of the invading armies survived. Israel spent the next three days gathering the wealth that the deceased soldiers had brought with them. God was still sovereign over the affairs of men!

We too can rest upon that truth in our lives. If we serve the Lord with the same heart that Jehoshaphat had in that situation, we can expect God to work out our battles to His glory. God may not perform a miracle, but we can trust that He will work things out for our best interests. As we have seen before, Romans 8:28 promises, *"And we know that all things work together for good to them that love God, to them who are the called according to his purpose."* As we go through life, we will face trials and difficulties that sometimes will seem insurmountable to us. The armies Israel faced in our passage seemed too powerful for them to defeat. In fact, they would have been too powerful for them…but not for God! Likewise, our trials are not a challenge to God. Proverbs 3:5, *"Trust in the LORD with all thine heart; and lean not unto thine own understanding."* We just need to learn to trust God completely and whenever we face a challenge in life, we need to turn to Him in prayer before doing anything else! What are you facing today? Is it a serious illness like cancer? Is it a major financial downturn that threatens you with losing your home? Is it a spouse that has decided they no longer have feelings for you? In all these seemingly desperate and insurmountable trials, we must first turn to the Lord! Sometimes our trials are the result of consequences of our own bad decisions, but in the end we have only one place to turn to. Romans 8:31 asks the question, *"What shall we then say to these things? If God be for us, who can be against us?"* The obvious answer should be that no one can stand against us! God is in control of all of it. Jehoshaphat knew this and we need to as well!

Half Dome, Yosemite, California, July 2007

# 48 – Fresh Bread!

In Jermiah 33:3 the Lord challenges us. He says, *"Call unto me, and I will answer thee, and shew thee great and mighty things, which thou knowest not."* In Matthew 21:22, the Lord Jesus promises us, *"And all things, whatsoever ye shall ask in prayer, believing, ye shall receive."* Over and over in the Scriptures we are told to pray to the God who can *"...do exceeding abundantly above all that we ask or think..."* (Ephesians 3:20). Through the shed blood of our Lord Jesus Christ, we have full and free access to God's throne in prayer. Hebrews 4:16 encourages us, *"Let us therefore come boldly unto the throne of grace, that we may obtain mercy, and find grace to help in time of need."*

A great illustration of God's provision in response to prayer comes from the life of George Müller. Müller was a preacher in England in the 1800s who established orphanages for the destitute children of that land. This account comes from the testimony of Abigail Townsend Luffe who was the child of one of Müller's associates (Steer, 1975, p.182). *"Early one morning Abigail was playing in Müller's garden on Ashley Down when he took her by the hand. 'Come, see what our Father will do.' He led her into a long dining room. The plates and cups or bowls were on the table. There was nothing on the table but empty dishes. There was no food in the larder, and no money to supply the need. The children were standing waiting for breakfast. 'Children, you know we must be in time for school,' said Müller. Then lifting his hand, he prayed, 'Dear Father, we thank Thee for what Thou art going to give us to eat.' According to the account, a knock was then heard at the door. The baker stood there. 'Mr. Müller, I couldn't sleep last night. Somehow, I felt you didn't have bread for breakfast, and the Lord wanted me to send you some. So, I got up at two o'clock and baked some fresh bread and have brought it.' Müller thanked the baker and praised God for His care. 'Children,' he said, 'we not only have bread, but the rare treat of fresh bread.' Almost immediately there came a second knock at the door. This time it was the milkman who announced that his milk cart had broken down outside the orphanage, and that he would like to give the children his cans of fresh milk, so that he could empty his wagon and repair it."*

Müller prayed about everything and expected an answer to every prayer…and he always got one! Müller was never a wealthy man; in fact, starting early in his ministry, he gave up any salary he received. He preferred to lift his needs to the Lord rather than resting on a worldly income. He never solicited donations from individuals but built and operated the orphanages entirely by faith. In his lifetime he cared for 10,024 orphans and the buildings to house them cost more than £100,000 but he built them in the 1800s without going a single penny in debt.

The story of Müller's life may seem extraordinary to us, but that is an indictment of our weak faith! We serve the same extraordinary God that Müller did! He can still do miraculously today if we trust Him and believe. In John 14:13, the Lord Jesus promises us, *"And whatsoever ye shall ask in my name, that will I do, that the Father may be glorified in the Son."* Go to the Lord in prayer over the needs in your life today and trust Him to provide for you and He will.

Pacific Coast Highway, California, July 2007

# 49 – He Increaseth Strength

We get tired sometimes…at least I know I do. Sometimes we can even get discouraged and think of quitting. When we get this way, we need to remember Isaiah 40:28-29. The prophet reminds us, *"²⁸Hast thou not known? hast thou not heard, that the everlasting God, the LORD, the Creator of the ends of the earth, fainteth not, neither is weary? there is no searching of his understanding. ²⁹He giveth power to the faint; and to them that have no might he increaseth strength."* These are some wonderful truths that should encourage us to stay faithful and keep serving the Lord! Isaiah begins by asking, haven't you known and heard about the Lord? We have the testimony of the Word of God for what He has done for the saints in the Old and New Testaments! We have two thousand years of Christian history to look back on to see how God provided! We can look back and see how God strengthened and encouraged each of them even in dire circumstances. Isaiah then points out that God is the Creator of all! If He made us, then He knows all about us and knows our needs so that we can trust Him. This Creator never wearies nor faints! He doesn't give up. He does not take a vacation. He does not sleep or even lose His concentration. He is always on watch, and nothing escapes His attention! We can trust Him completely! He is also the all-knowing, all-powerful, loving and wise God! There is nothing we can face that He hasn't accounted for. He knows the end from the beginning. The enemy cannot come up with a scheme He has not foreseen. This is the God we serve!

It is this God that gives power to the faint and increases our strength when we are weak! When the Apostle Paul was struggling, the Lord spoke to Him. 2 Corinthians 12:9, *"And he said unto me, My grace is sufficient for thee: for my strength is made perfect in weakness. Most gladly therefore will I rather glory in my infirmities, that the power of Christ may rest upon me."* He goes on in the last part of the next verse to say, *"...for when I am weak, then am I strong."* We suffer from weakness in this flesh, but in the spirit, through Christ, we can have great strength. That strength is not of ourselves, but of God. When we trust in our own strength, it will fail, but God gives us strength to go beyond what we can endure in ourselves. Verse 31 of our passage in Isaiah is well known. The prophet says, *"But they that wait upon the LORD shall renew their strength; they shall mount up with wings as eagles; they shall run, and not be weary; and they shall walk, and not faint."* God is our inexhaustible wellspring of strength to do what He wants us to do. God always provides for those who trust in Him. Those who trust Him and wait upon Him will soar with eagle's wings through the trials of life. Again, in Psalm 27:14, we are told, *"Wait on the LORD: be of good courage, and he shall strengthen thine heart: wait, I say, on the LORD."* As we wait on the Lord and trust in Him, we will receive the strength we need to get through each day!

# 50 – The Desires of Thine Heart

God wants to give you every desire of your heart! Right?! Well, yes and no. Our Bible Gem for today comes from Psalm 37:4-5. Here God's Word says, *"⁴Delight thyself also in the LORD; and he shall give thee the desires of thine heart. ⁵Commit thy way unto the LORD; trust also in him; and he shall bring it to pass."* I have heard prosperity preachers take these verses out of context to teach that God gives us anything we want simply because we are His children! After all, God wants to be happy, doesn't He? He wants to *"give thee the desires of thine heart!"* That is absolutely incorrect! Well, mostly it is! There is much more to these verses than they are teaching.

First, this promise is conditional. The conditions are to *"Delight thyself...in the LORD..." "Commit thy way unto the LORD..."* and *"trust...in him..."* When we delight ourselves in the Lord and in His Word, God will give us the desires of our heart in two ways. The first way is that we will be desiring the things that please God when we delight ourselves in Him. God literally places the desires in our heart for the things He wants for us. If it is God who gives us those desires then secondly, He gives those things to us and thus fulfills those desires as well. If you delight yourself in the Lord, you are going to seek His will for your life. You are going to stand for righteousness. You are going to desire to be close to Him. You are going to search for opportunities to serve Him. He will gladly give you those things! If, on the other hand, you delight yourself in the things of the world, you might want a brand-new Ferrari to take people to church in. God is probably not so inclined to give you that desire because it reveals the worldliness of your heart, and you aren't truly delighting in Him. God is not here promising to give us a lavish lifestyle, but that He will give us the things that promote godliness. James 4:3 says, *"Ye ask, and receive not, because ye ask amiss, that ye may consume it upon your lusts."* If you want worldly things to fulfill your carnal desires, God does not promise them to you, and you will likely not receive them. 1 John 5:14, however, tells us what we can have confidence in regarding God's provision. It reads, *"And this is the confidence that we have in him, that, if we ask any thing according to his will, he heareth us:"* God's fulfillment of our desires is according to His will. If we desire His will, then we can have confidence in His perfect provision.

So, then the promise of Psalm 37:4-5 is a promise that as you seek God with all your heart and delight in His presence, then He promises to give you your heart's desires because you will want exactly what He wants for you. Do you want God to give you the desires of your heart? Then fall in love with Him, immerse yourself in His Word, and serve Him faithfully among God's people in His house, the church. Learn to delight yourself in the things of God and He will fulfill His will in your life.

# 51 – What Must I Do to Be Saved?

Paul and Silas were roughly handled and arrested for their ministry in the city of Phillippi. There they were thrown in a prison for the terrible crime of preaching salvation through Christ! The intention of the magistrates was to intimidate the two preachers and silence their ministry for good. ...but God had other plans! Acts 16:25 records, *"And at midnight Paul and Silas prayed, and sang praises unto God: and the prisoners heard them."* Paul and Silas would not be silenced by intimidation and while in the deep dark dungeon they sang and praised God in voices loud enough for everyone to hear them in the middle of the night. In the next verse God sends a midnight earthquake to free them from their bonds! The jailer, afraid of losing his prisoners prepared to kill himself, but Paul encouraged and assured him that they were not going anywhere. The jailer came trembling to the preachers, *"And brought them out, and said, Sirs, what must I do to be saved?"* (verse 30). Now, I don't know if the jailer fully understood what he was asking. He may have been concerned about the situation and what would happen if the prisoners chose to flee...or he may have been referring to the things that Paul and Silas had been preaching. Regardless, Paul and Silas respond in verse 31. *"And they said, Believe on the Lord Jesus Christ, and thou shalt be saved, and thy house."* What the jailer received in response to his question was the saving message of Jesus Christ! The jailer took them into his home and the preachers gave the Gospel message to the jailer and all those in his house…and they believed on Jesus Christ! They received the promise of Romans 10:13, *"For whosoever shall call upon the name of the Lord shall be saved."* They by faith believed on Jesus Christ as their Saviour and received God's blessed gift of eternal salvation.

Have you ever believed on the Lord Jesus Christ for your salvation? Acts 4:12 says, *"Neither is there salvation in any other: for there is none other name under heaven given among men, whereby we must be saved."* The Lord Jesus is the only One who can save you from your sin! Romans 3:23 says, *"For all have sinned, and come short of the glory of God;"* We are all nothing more than sinners who have been separated from God. No matter how good we may be, we have all violated God's law at some point! We now stand guilty before Him. Romans 6:23 tells us the consequences of our sin! *"For the wages of sin is death…"* There is a death sentence against us for our sin! And this is not just physical death, but something more! Revelation 20:14 warns, *"And death and hell were cast into the lake of fire. This is the second death."* There is spiritual death which means a person is separated from God forever in the awful flames of Hell and the Lake of Fire! But Romans 6:23 doesn't end there. It goes on to promise, *"…but the gift of God is eternal life through Jesus Christ our Lord."* We don't have to die and go to Hell, because Jesus Christ took our punishment when He died in our place on the cross! Romans 5:8 says, *"But God commendeth his love toward us, in that, while we were yet sinners, Christ died for us.*" We were the guilty sinners, but Christ died in our place! Since He was God in the flesh, His blood was of infinite value and so He can offer that payment that He made to any and all who come to Him by faith! You must trust in what Jesus did on the cross for you and not in anything you do! Doing good deeds, getting baptized, being a member of a church are all good things, but none of them have anything to do with saving your soul! You must understand from the Word of God that you are a Hell deserving sinner who is unable to redeem him or herself. You must then understand that Jesus Christ died for your sin. Then simply ask God to save you because of what Christ did for you. The prayer does not save you, but it is the faith in your heart that God is looking for. Do that today and know, *"For whosoever shall call upon the name of the Lord shall be saved."* Trust in the Lord as your Saviour today and you will receive God's gift of eternal life. You have God's Word on it!!!

If you have any questions or want to learn more about salvation, please call Lighthouse Baptist Church at 502-531-0534. We would be glad to tell you how to be saved and help you as you begin your new Christian life!

Sunset over Monument Valley, Arizona, July 2007

# 52 – He Prayed for Us!

I am praying for you! We say that to people all the time. Sadly, this really is not true but just something a person says to try to be an encouragement. At other times it is a serious commitment we make to lift that individual up before the Throne of Grace. I try never to say that I will pray for someone unless I truly am going to do so. In the Bible we find that there are many prayers recorded for us. The one that I consider to be among the most precious is in John chapter 17. In this chapter, we have what is the Lord's prayer for Himself and His disciples, just hours before He went to Calvary's cross. It has been called the Lord's high priestly prayer. What is so special about it in my view is found in verse 20. Here the Lord not only prays for the disciples that were present there, but for others who we will identify in a moment. That will be an encouragement to us! He prays, *"Neither pray I for these alone, but for them also which shall believe on me through their word;"* That's us today! Our Lord Jesus prayed for you and me! This was one of the very last prayers the Lord prayed during His earthly life and ministry, and He is praying for us! His thoughts were toward us the night before He died, but more than that, we were on His mind while He was on the cross. Hebrews 12:2 informs us, *"Looking unto Jesus the author and finisher of our faith; who for the joy that was set before him endured the cross, despising the shame, and is set down at the right hand of the throne of God."* Christ suffered on the cross while looking toward the final result, which was our salvation!

He is a Redeemer that can relate to us and to whom we can relate because He took on human flesh to live the only righteous life ever lived. We do not worship a distant Saviour who cannot relate to us! In Hebrews 4:15, we are told, *"For we have not an high priest which cannot be touched with the feeling of our infirmities; but was in all points tempted like as we are, yet without sin."* The next verse then encourages us that because of this, *"Let us therefore come boldly unto the throne of grace, that we may obtain mercy, and find grace to help in time of need."* We have an approachable Saviour, and we can come to Him in our times of need.

This is our Saviour who prayed for us 2,000 years ago. We are still receiving the benefit of that answered prayer today. This should be an encouragement to every believer in Christ! We can have a personal relationship with the One who redeemed us! His Holy Spirit dwells with us and in us! In John 14:17, the Lord Jesus gives us this promise, *"Even the Spirit of truth; whom the world cannot receive, because it seeth him not, neither knoweth him: but ye know him; for he dwelleth with you, and shall be in you."*

In his prayer in John 17, the Lord Jesus prays for our sanctification and our witness. He prays for our unity in Christ through the truth of God's Word. How loving and caring is our Saviour toward us! It was His love that caused Him to pray for us and it was His love that led Him to die for our sins. In 1 John 4:9 it says, *"In this was manifested the love of God toward us, because that God sent his only begotten Son into the world, that we might live through him."* As the hymn writer C. Austin Miles wrote in 1912, *"And He walks with me, and He talks with me, And He tells me I am His own, And the joy we share as we tarry there, None other, has ever, known!!"* Our Saviour does walk with us and commune with us through our Christian life. The last part of Hebrews 13:5 reminds us of His promise, *"...for he hath said, I will never leave thee, nor forsake thee."* Our Lord can be relied on, and He loves us. This should help us go through life and should encourage us to live for Him every day!

Watkins Glen, New York, October 2007

# **Conclusion**

I always closed my short radio broadcast by saying, "Keep studying the Word and before long you will be finding your own Bible Gems!" That is the message I want to give you here. I have shared a few thoughts that God has given me through His Word. By carefully studying the Bible for yourself, God can similarly speak to your heart and give you many insights that apply directly to your life and ministry. It is a great blessing when God speaks to us in that way, and I hope you will invest the time and effort that it takes for you to find your own Bible Gems!

Mammoth Cave, Kentucky, January 2020

# References

Anxiety and Depression Association of America. (2024). *Anxiety Disorders: Facts & Statistics*. Retrieved from https://adaa.org/understanding-anxiety/facts-statistics

Crosby, Fanny. (1894). *My Savior First of All*. Publisher Unknown (Public Domain).

Lemmel, Hellen Howarth. (1922). *Turn Your Eyes upon Jesus*. Publisher Unknown (Public Domain).

Murray, Andrew. (1897). *Absolute Surrender.* New York, New York: Fleming H. Revell Company,

Meigs, Charles. (1917). *Others*. Publisher Unknown (Public Domain).

Miles, C. Austin. (1912). *In the Garden*. Publisher Unknown (Public Domain).

Mohler, R. Albert. (2016). *The Scandal of Biblical Illiteracy: It's Our Problem.* Retrieved from https://albertmohler.com/2016/01/20/the-scandal-of-biblical-illiteracy-its-our-problem-4/

Studd, Charles (C.T.). (1884). *Only One Life, Twill Soon Be Past*. Publisher Unknown (Public Domain).

Steer, Roger. (1975). *George Müller: Delighted in God.* Wheaton, IL: Harold Shaw Publishers.

United Nations (UN). (2017). *UN health agency reports depression now 'leading cause of disability worldwide.'* Retrieved from https://news.un.org/en/story/2017/02/552062.

Webster, Noah. (1828). *American Dictionary of the English Language.* San Francisco, CA: Foundation for American Christian Education.

Bill and Elaine, Linderhof Palace, Germany, May 2014

Preserving Our Baptist History

# Other books by Bill Delperdange

### How Can I Understand It? How to Study and Understand Your Bible

Many people struggle to understand the Word of God. This book is intended to be a resource to help them. We subconsciously recognize the rules of interpretation when we read other literature but then struggle when it comes to reading the Bible. The rules for reading a fiction novel are different from the rules for reading a newspaper. We do not give thought to the differences but understand them naturally. This book seeks to help people properly apply the appropriate rules of interpretation to the Word of God to aid in comprehension. This book will be a help to anyone seeking to understand their Bible.

Available on Amazon: https://amzn.to/4ghiTKg

### Exploring God's Word Series:

### Treasures in Romans: A Romans Commentary

The Epistle of Paul to the Romans in the New Testament was written by the Apostle to teach the church basic sound doctrine. Salvation is the focus of the epistle, but Paul covers everything from eschatology to interactions with worldly government. Romans is one of the most important doctrinal books of the Bible.

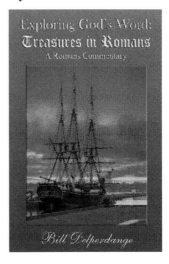

Available on Amazon:
https://amzn.to/3UprlOe

### To Live for Christ: New Believer's Discipleship

To Live for Christ, New Believer's Discipleship, is a twelve-week basic discipleship class for new believers in Christ. The class is formatted for a twelve-week duration which can be repeated so that students can enter the class in any week and complete the material over the following twelve weeks. Each class is independent, so the order of the lessons can be changed as desired.

Teacher's Edition Available on Amazon: https://amzn.to/3ARxxaN

Student's Edition Available on Amazon: https://amzn.to/4dPJgVZ

### Three Men That Changed the World: The Baptists and American Liberty

Shubal Stearns, Samuel Harriss, and John Leland are three Baptist preachers that the world has largely forgotten. Even among Baptists they are not widely known. Yet these three men were instrumental in establishing the freedoms we hold dear. This is the story of three Baptist preachers that changed the world!

Available on Amazon:
https://amzn.to/4h6YhDZ

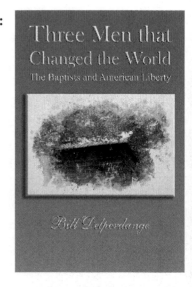

# Please visit me on YouTube:

https://www.youtube.com/PreservingOurBaptistHistory

Email me at: preserving.our.baptist.history@gmail.com

Visit my SpreadShop:

https://preserving-our-baptist-histor.myspreadshop.com/

Listen to great Christian radio on your phone with the WIOP Radio app (in the App Store) or listen online at: https://www.lighthousebaptistkjv1611.com/wiop-radio

If you are in the Shepherdsville, KY, area we are on your radio at 95.1 FM.

# About the Author

Bill Delperdange was born in New Jersey but raised in upstate New York near Rochester. In the 1980s he enlisted in the United States Air Force and was trained as an aircraft mechanic. In 1991, he was stationed at RAF Mildenhall in England. It was here that he trusted in Christ as his personal Saviour on April 15, 1992. Bill graduated from Bethany Bible College in Dothan, Alabama in

*Bill Delperdange*
*MSgt. USAF. Retired*

June of 2000 with a Bachelor of Arts in (Pastoral) Ministry. He spent a brief time working as a missionary in Tokyo, Japan, and then was on staff at Maranatha Baptist Church in Lyons, NY, under

*Bill and Elaine Delperdange*

the ministry of Pastor Rodger Bottrell. In 2015, Bill and his lovely wife, Elaine, moved to Louisville, KY, and became members of Lighthouse Baptist Church in Shepherdsville, KY. At the end of 2022, Bill left secular employment to accept a position of Director of Lighthouse Institute of the Bible and Lighthouse Baptist Missions Field Director (under the leadership of Pastor David Jordan). He also operates the Preserving Our Baptist History YouTube channel.

Made in the USA
Columbia, SC
07 February 2025

52720227R00076